AMERICAN
HALF-TRACKS
of
WORLD WAR 2

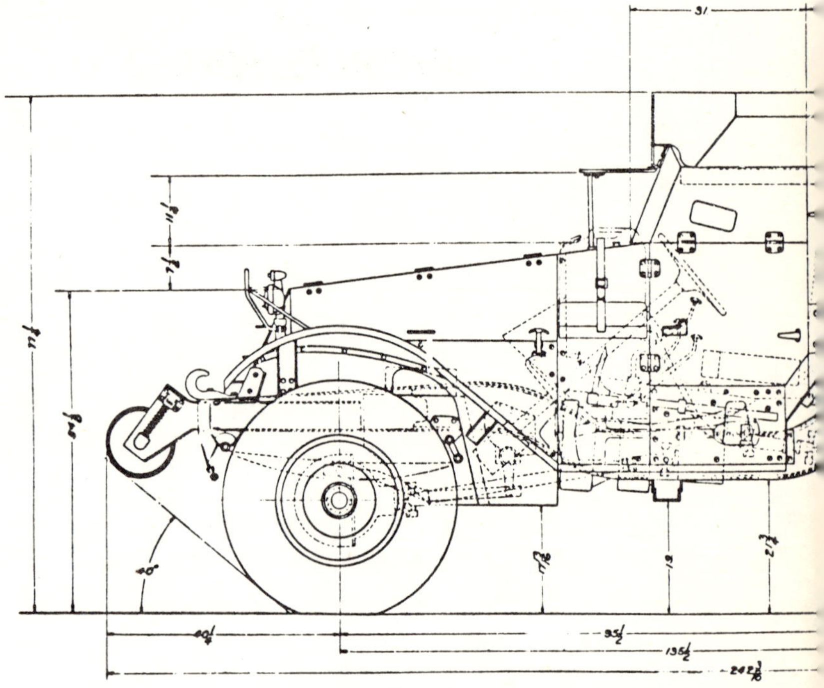

This is a miniature reproduction of a complete sheet of official US Ordnance Department drawings which were prepared for the major half-track production variants, in this case the M9A1. Further reproductions are included at the end of the text section in this book.

AMERICAN HALF-TRACKS
of
WORLD WAR 2

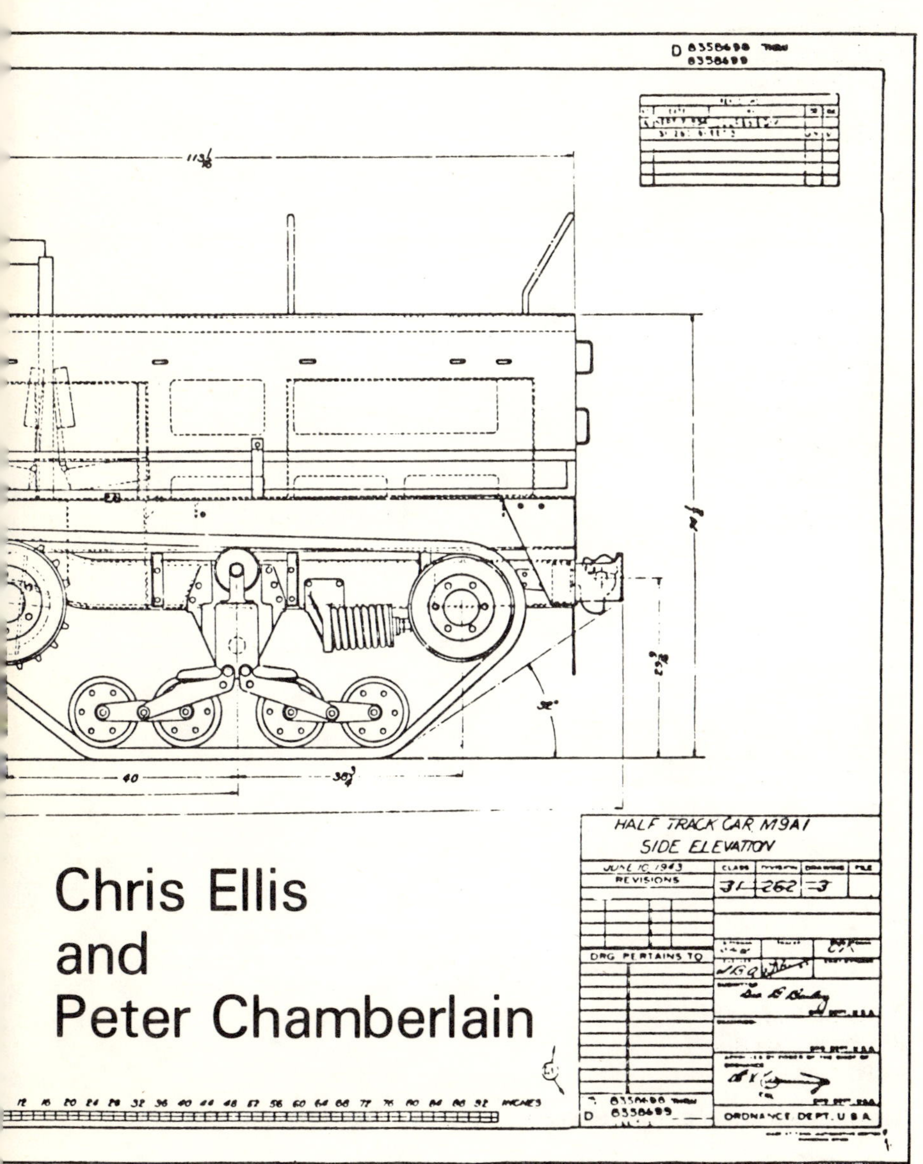

Chris Ellis
and
Peter Chamberlain

Bellona Publications,
Argus Books Ltd.
14 St. James Road,
Watford, Herts,
England

First Published 1978

ISBN 0 85242 581 3

Typeset in England by
Reprologo, Leatherhead,
Surrey

Printed and bound in England by Staples Printers Ltd., Love Lane, Rochester, Kent.

PREFACE

H A L F - T R A C K vehicles have always exerted a strong fascination for military vehicle enthusiasts, and the half-track was very much a product of automotive technology of the 1930s and 1940s. The Germans were the first to use half-tracks on a grand scale for military use, finding in the concept a good compromise between fast road running and effective cross-country performance, and the sturdy chassis and suspension would also support the weight of an armoured body when the vehicle was developed as an infantry carrier. The French developed their own range of military half-tracks in the 1930s, based mostly on the ideas of Citroen. The US Army kept a close watch on developments in Europe and the new family of half-tracks developed around 1940 was similar to the German half-track idea in concept but was more closely based on the much simpler French Citroen-Kégresse in running gear.

As it happened the development of the US Army half-track was timely, for the basic design (built by several manufacturing concerns) proved to be very enduring, reliable, and stable. It lent itself to a huge number of special purpose adaptations, few of which had been foreseen or envisaged in 1940 when the basic vehicle was designed. Produced in huge numbers, it served the US Army and her Allies in all theatres of war and for all sorts of duty from troop carrier to ambulance.

But even by 1944 it was considered that the half-track had had its day. The US Army decided to replace half-tracks with full-track carriers, but had hardly begun to do so before the war ended.

In the next few years, however, all new carrier designs by the major powers were of either full-track or all-wheel type and there has never been any subsequent American half-track model. The wartime US half-tracks have soldiered on well into the 1970s with some armies, notably the Israeli Defence Forces, and a surprising number still give remarkably good service a full generation after half-track production ceased in America!

This book provides an easy to-follow reference guide to the development and output of the many American half-track models produced. As far as possible, the text is kept in chronological order, allowing, of course, for grouping by type. In the pictorial section we have attempted to show every known model or variant of significance, with only minor variants omitted. The pictures, again, are presented as nearly as possible in chronological order. Small reproductions of official US Ordnance Department drawings of some models are also included.

For assistance in tracking down illustrations and information we are grateful to Colonel R. J. Icks, AUS (Rtd), Major J. Loop, AUS, Bart H. Vanderveen, and J. Lucas, and G. Pavey, of the Imperial War Museum, London. Photograph sources include the US Army, Imperial War Museum, Icks Collection, Vanderveen Collection, and Chamberlain Collection.

Peter Chamberlain/Chris Ellis

CONTENTS

CHAPTER ONE

INTRODUCTION

DURING 1925, the United States Ordnance Department purchased from the French car manufacturer, Citroen, two semi-tracked vehicles that the Citroen firm had developed in collaboration with Alexander Kégresse who had pioneered this type of vehicle during 1911. The two vehicles that were purchased were tested at the Aberdeen Proving Ground as prime movers for the 75 mm field gun.

In 1931, a further vehicle of modified design, a Citroen-Kégresse P.17, was procured for tests and evaluation. Due to the excellent results shown by this vehicle, further development was undertaken by American commercial motor firms for the US Ordnance Department. The first American-built half-track vehicle was designed by James Cunningham, Son and Co; this was tested as a reconnaisance car by the Ordnance Department, and designated Half-Track Car T1. Modified versions of this vehicle were produced at the Rock Island Arsenal and designated T1E1 (M1), T1E2, T1E3. Meanwhile, development of a slightly different type of vehicle, the Half-Track Truck T1, by General Motors was authorised in 1933. This was followed by various other half-track trucks developed specifically as cargo carriers or as prime movers for artillery, with designation from T2 to T9. In the later Half-Track Truck T9, built in 1937 by the Marmon-Herrington Company for the Ordnance Department, first use was made of front wheel drive synchronised with the bogie drive. This vehicle was standardised as Half-Track Truck M2.

The final significant development of this period was the conversion of a wheeled Scout Car, M2A1, into a half-track vehicle by the White Motor Company and Rock Island Arsenal in 1938. The front axle drive of the Scout Car was retained and a volute spring type rear suspension, as used on the Half-Track Truck, M2 was installed. This hybrid vehicle was designated Half-Track Personnel Carrier, T7.

As the performance of this vehicle proved satisfactory further development of this type of vehicle was authorised in December 1939, on the recommendation of the Mechanised Cavalry Board. This work was carried out by the Diamond T Motor Company, who developed an improved version of the T7, designated Half-Track Scout Car T14. This vehicle was the prototype of the standard half-track cars and carriers used in World War 2. It was standardised in September 1940 as Half-Track Car M2. Equipped internally with extra seats for the transportation of 14

Summary of early half-track development models

Designation	Year	Remarks
Citroen-Kégresse Tractor P.17	1930	Same as French Army Vehicle.
Half-Track Car, T1	1931	Built by J. Cunningham, Son and Co.
Half-Track Car, T1E1	1933	Rebuilt T1; 30 made at Rock Island Arsenal.
Half-Track Car, T1E2	1933	Rebuilt T1; rubber jointed track.
Half-Track Car, T1E3	1935	Rebuilt T1E2, with volute springs.
Half-Track Car, T2		Design Study Only
Half-Track Truck, T1	1933	GMC $2\frac{1}{2}$ ton truck with half-track unit from T1E2 and rubber band track. Six more ordered then cancelled.
Half-Track Truck, T2	1933	Cunningham $1\frac{1}{2}$ ton truck (Ford $1\frac{1}{2}$ ton truck with Cunningham half-track unit similar to that on T1E1); later with Cunningham Oilite Bushed Track.
Cunningham-Chevrolet Half-Track Truck	1933	Chevrolet 1 ton truck with Cunningham needle bearing track of rubber blocks
Half-Track Truck, T3	1933	Linn WD 12 Tractor with engine replaced by American La France 12 cylinder engine.
Half-Track Truck, T4	1934	GMC truck with Cunningham unit similar to Half-Track Truck T1.
Half-Track Truck, T4E1		Specification only, for Signal Corps wire laying truck.
Half-Track Truck, T5	1935	GMC built. Similar to Half-Track Truck T1. Originally 8-inch track later 10 inch; 24 built
Half-Track Truck, T5E1	1935	T5 modified, with rear axle reduction ratio increased.
Half-Track Truck, T5E2	1938	T5E1 with 10 inch track and larger bogie wheels; Cunningham rubber block track.
Half-Track Truck, T6	1934	Linn; smaller than Half-Track Truck T3 cancelled after one made.
Half-Track Truck, T7		Specification only for medium artillery prime mover.
Half-Track Truck, T8	1935	1935 Ford $1\frac{1}{2}$ ton truck with Trackson cable track unit. Failed military tests.
Half-Track Truck, T9	1936	1936 Ford with volute spring half-track unit and Marmon-Herrington front wheel unit, 4 bogie wheel unit and T21 tracks (Rubber block rubber bushed).
Half-Track Truck, T9E1	1936	Same with two wheeled bogie and T20E2 track.
Production, T9	1937	Same but 1937 Ford chassis and rubber band tracks T24E1. Two built.
Production, T9E1	1937	Same but 1937 Ford chassis and T24E1 track.
Half-Track Truck, T9E2	1935	Pilot T9E1 with pneumatic tyred bogie wheels. Returned to original form after tests.
Half-Track Truck, T10		Specification only, Light half-track wire laying truck.
Half-Track Truck, T16		Diamond T made prime mover for 105mm Howitzer.
Half-Track Truck, T17		White made.
Half-Track Truck, T17 Modified		Cupola added.
Half-Track Truck, T19		Built by Mack, engine at rear.
Half Track Truck, T3		Built by Mack.

men, the chassis was standardised as the Half-Track Personnel Carrier M3. While both the M2 and M3 were similar in design and appearance and interchangeable in major assemblies, the two vehicles differed in tactical use. The M2 car was a prime mover for artillery up to the 155 mm howitzer, and served as an armoured reconnaissance vehicle. The M3 carrier, while primarily a personnel carrier for armoured divisions and motorised artillery, served also as an ambulance, radio carrier, prime mover for artillery and as the basis for a self-propelled gun mount. In practice the distinction between the two in tactical employment swiftly disappeared when America went to war in December 1941.

The first orders for half-track vehicles were placed under the US Ordnance Department's long established peacetime system of competitive bidding. Bids were submitted by various companies, notably the Autocar Company, the White Motor Company, the pioneer in this field, who were already making the M2A1 Scout Car, and the Diamond T Motor Company. As the Autocar Co submitted the lowest bid, they were awarded a contract to make 424 Half-Track Cars, M2, in September 1940. This was followed with a contract to the Diamond T Co to develop the Half-Track Personnel Carrier M3. As increased requirements for the half-tracks M2 and M3 made manufacture by any one company impossible save by a large expansion of facilities, it was agreed by Autocar, White and Diamond T that all vehicles made by these companies under the supervision of the Ordnance Department would be standardised, having interchangeable components.

Early in 1942, overall requirements for half-tracks were substantially increased. Not only were the manufacturing facilities then engaged in half-track production inadequate to meet the increased demand, but components facilities were also at the limit of their production. It now became necessary to obtain a new source for making these vehicles and their components. Steps were thus taken to use the production facilities of the International Harvester Company, the well-known tractor makers. At this time changes were made in the design of the vehicles and those produced by International Harvester Company (IHC) embodied all changes released at that time for the previous models. The vehicles made by International Harvester were designated Half-Track Personnel Carrier M5 and Half-Track Car M9. These were basically similar to Half-Track Personnel Carrier M3 and Half-Track Car M2, but featured IHC components including an International Red 450 B engine. The body was of homogenous armour plate and a distinctive external feature was the rounded rear corners of the IHC vehicles. The M2 and M3 had face-hardened armour and squared-off rear corners to the body. IHC vehicles were fitted with rear doors.

Two general development projects were contemplated during 1942 and 1943. A so-called $\frac{3}{4}$-track model was begun in early 1942; the rear suspension unit was lengthened and other improved features were incorporated, all under the designations Half-Track Trucks T16, T17 and T19. This was intended to reduce the space between the rear suspension mechanism and the front wheels, which produced high front axle loading and a tendency to hang and strain the vehicle on rough terrain. Tests were successful, but the decision of the Field Artillery to concentrate on high speed tractors as prime movers for artillery resulted in loss of interest in these heavy-duty half-track trucks.

Development of a universal body half-track vehicle, to combine all military requirements for personnel carriers was begun in April 1943. A half-track combining the essential features of the M2 and M3 was accordingly developed and designated Half-Track Car T29. This vehicle was standardised in October 1943 as the M3A2. A similar project for consolidating the M5 and M9 in one basic model resulted in Half-Track Car T31. This was adopted as substitute standard and re-designated Half-Track Car M5A2. Curtailment of the half-track programme began in mid-1943, however, and further limitations were made at the end of 1943. There was no new production except re-manufacturing programmes of the M2, M9A1 cars, and M3 and M5 carriers beyond 1943, and no production of the M2 car and the M5A1 carrier beyond 1944. Complete total built was 41,169 vehicles. Half-track production was, in fact, terminated with the idea of concentrating on full-track vehicles for all the roles which the half-track fulfilled, ie, troop carrier, SP mount, and prime mover. However, due to demand in the field and development delays the half-track remained a widely used vehicle in the US Army until the end of the war in 1945.

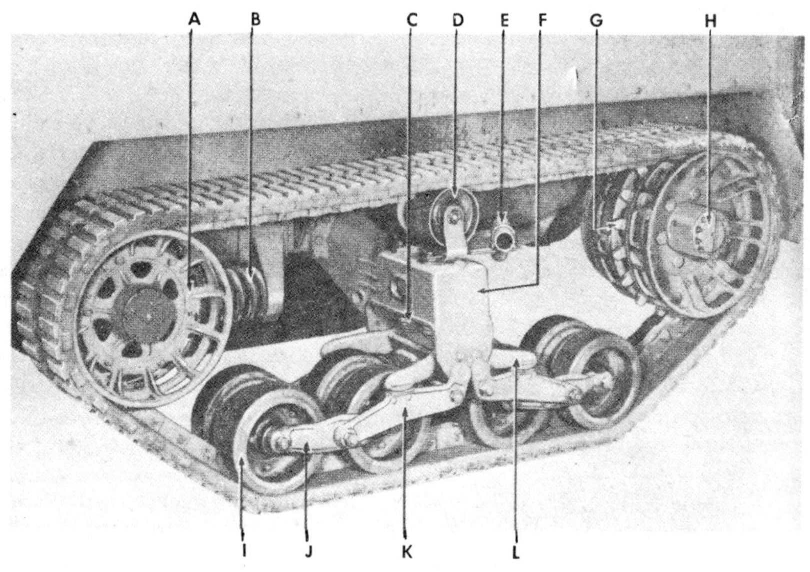

A—IDLER WHEEL
B—IDLER SPRING
C—VOLUTE SPRING
D—BOGIE UPPER ROLLER
E—TAIL PIPE
F—BOGIE AND FRAME ASSEMBLY
G—TRACK DRIVING SPROCKET
H—REAR AXLE SHAFT FLANGE
I—BOGIE ROLLER
J—BOGIE FRAME
K—BOGIE ARM
L—CRAB

Bogie and track details, standard for all vehicles.

CHAPTER TWO

PERSONNEL CARRIERS

P R O D U C T I O N preparations for the first standardised half-track design started in late 1940 with first vehicle deliveries planned for spring and early summer of 1941. Numerous models were developed, all superficially alike but actually varying considerably in detail and fittings. Here they are described in detail, keeping as nearly as possible to chronological order.

Half-Track Car, M2: The first Half-Track Cars, M2, were accepted from Autocar and White in May of 1941. Total production of this vehicle was 11,415, with 2,992 produced by Autocar and 8,423 by White under the mutually agreed joint building scheme.

This vehicle had seats for a crew of ten, plus a driver's seat, commander's seat and one passenger seat in the driving compartment. A skate rail surrounded the interior of the vehicle and by the use of two carriage mounts, a cal .30 and cal .50 machine gun could be moved along this rail and fired in any direction. There was no rear door on this model, and two large ammunition storage compartments with outside doors were located behind the driver's compartment. A lid on each storage chest opened from inside the vehicle allowing removal of ammunition boxes from the top shelf. Access to the remaining shelves was reached from outside the vehicle. The fuel tanks were placed inside the vehicle at the rear sides. A radio mast was located at the side of the rear centre seat. There were no rifle racks or gun pedestals on this version. Armament consisted of one .30 and one .50 calibre machine gun and a .45 calibre machine carbine. There was either a roller or winch at the front of the vehicle. This vehicle was also used as a prime mover for the 105 mm howitzer.

Brief details: Weight 19,800 lb (gross); Crew 10; Armour $\frac{1}{4}$ inch all round except windshield protective plate $\frac{1}{2}$ inch; Length, with roller 19 ft 6 $\frac{1}{4}$ ins, with winch 20 ft 1 5/8 ins; Height 7 ft 5 ins; Width, with mine-racks 7 ft 3 $\frac{1}{2}$ ins, without mine racks 6 ft 5 $\frac{1}{4}$ ins; Engine, White 160AX 6 cylinder 148 hp; Speed 40 mph; Range 175 miles; Ammunition stowage, Cal .50, 700 rds, Cal .30, 7,750 rds, Cal .45, 540 rds; Mine stowage, 14.

Half-Track Car, T16: This was an M2, with a strengthened suspension, and fitted with an armoured roof. It was experimental only, produced early in 1942. It was later designated M2E1.

Half-Track Car, M2E2: This was an M2 experimentally fitted with International Harvester Company components to develop the IHC-built M9.

Half-Track Car, M3E3: This was a further modified M2E2.

Half-Track Car, M2E4: This was an experimental model of the M2, fitted with a Hercules diesel engine.

Half-Track Car, M2E5: This was a basic M2 fitted with International Harvester Co components and acted as a final prototype for the M9.

Half-Track Car, M2E6: This was a standard Half-Track Car, M2, modified by the addition of the .50 cal anti-aircraft circular ring mount and three socket mounts for a cal .30 machine gun, eliminating the skate rail. It became the pilot model of the M2A1, M3A1, M5A1, and M9A1. The A1 designation was added to each basic half-track model incorporating these improvements.

Half-Track Car, M2A1: Production of the modified model, M2A1, was begun in October, 1943, and a total of 1,643 vehicles was accepted by the termination of production in March 1944. This version was similar to the M2, but had the M49 gun ring mount for a cal .50 machine gun over the co-driver's seat, for use against low-flying aircraft and ground targets. Three fixed pintle sockets were mounted, one on each side and one at the rear of the body, permitting the use of a cal .30 machine gun.

Half-Track Car, M2, with Mine Exploder: One M2 half-track was experimentally modified as an anti-personnel mine clearing vehicle with a light girder structure and flail carried ahead of the bonnet. The flail was operated from the engine.

Half-Track Personnel Carrier, M3: The first Half-Track Personnel Carrier M3 was procured from Autocar with later production by Diamond T and White. First deliveries were in May of 1941 and total production was 12,499 vehicles. This vehicle was generally similar to the M2, but had seating accommodation for 13 men. There were three seats in the driver's compartment, the other ten being arranged in two rows of five, each backed up against the fuel tanks and body sides. The fuel tanks were located just behind the driver's compartment, at the side of the vehicle. The body was ten inches longer than that of the M2, and had a door at the rear. There was no radio mast or skate rail fitted to this model, but a M25 pedestal mount for a .50 calibre machine gun was secured to the floor, just behind the centre seat of the driving compartment. Rifle racks for six rifles each side were fitted along the sides in the space at the back of the side seats.

The M3 was also used in the role of ambulance, radio carrier, and prime mover for artillery. With further modifications the chassis was adapted for various gun motor carriages. Brief details: Weight, 20,000 lb (gross); Crew, 13; Armour, $\frac{1}{4}$ inch all round except windshield protective plate, $\frac{1}{2}$ inch; Length with roller, 20 ft 3 $\frac{1}{2}$ ins, with winch, 20 ft 95/8 ins; Height, 7 ft 5 ins; Width, with mine racks, 7 ft 3 $\frac{1}{2}$ ins, without mine racks, 6 ft 5 $\frac{1}{4}$ ins; Engine, White 160AX 6 cylinder 148 hp; Speed, 40 mph; Cross-country, 35 mph; Range, 175 miles; Ammunition stowage, Cal .50, 700 rds, Cal .30, 4,000 rds, Cal .45, 540 rds; Mine stowage, 24.

Half-Track Personnel Carrier, M3A1: This was similar to the M3, but had a M49 ring mount for a cal .50 machine gun over the co-driver's seat. Three pintle sockets, for cal .30 machine guns were fitted, one each side and one at the rear of the vehicle.

Production of the M3A1 was begun in October 1943 and a total of 2,862 vehicles were accepted from Diamond T.

Half-Track Personnel Carrier, M3E2: This was an M3 experimentally fitted with International Harvester Company components to become the prototype for the IHC-built M5.

Half-Track Car, M3A2 (T29): This was a modification of the Half-Track Personnel Carrier M3A1 designed to replace the Half-Track Personnel Carriers M3 and M3A1 and Half-Track Car M2 and M2A1. Development of a multi-purpose Universal half-track to fulfil all military requirements for personnel carriers was begun by International Harvester Company in March 1943. A half-track combining the essential features of the M2 and M3 was developed by July 1943 and designated Half-Track Car T29. This vehicle was considered satisfactory by the Armored Board and was standardised in October 1943 as the M3A2. Variations in stowage arrangements, through the use of suitable removable lockers, enabled the vehicle to perform a variety of duties. Crews ranged from five to 12 men, depending on the amount of stowage carried and the tactical purpose intended. Three pintle sockets were provided and a demountable ring mount M49 for a cal .50 machine gun was erected above the co-driver's seat. A one-piece armour shield was fitted to protect the machine gunner. When used as a machine gun carrier, additional ammunition was carried in place of two of the seats.

Brief details: Weight, 21,200 lb (gross); Crew, 5 to 12; Armour, $\frac{1}{4}$ inch all round except for windshield protective plate, $\frac{1}{2}$ inch; Length, with roller, 20 ft 3 $\frac{1}{2}$ ins, without winch, 20 ft 9 5/8 ins; Height, 6 ft 5 $\frac{3}{4}$ ins; Width, with mine-racks, 7 ft 3 $\frac{1}{2}$ ins, without mine-racks, 6 ft 5 $\frac{1}{4}$ ins; Engine, White 160AX 6 cylinder 148 hp; Speed, 40 mph; Range, 175 miles; Ammunition stowage, Cal .50, 330 rds, Cal .30, 2,000 rds, Cal .45, 180 rds; Mine stowage, 24.

Half-Track Car, M3A3: A modified version of M3A2 with detail changes.

Half-Track Car M3A4: A further modified version of the M3A2 with a larger ring mount.

Half-Track Personnel Carrier, M5: Similar to the Half-Track Personnel Carrier M3, this vehicle was manufactured by the International Harvester Company, and incorporated that company's component parts. It was powered by an International Red 450B 6 cylinder 4-cycle in-line gasoline engine. Body armour was of homogeneous armour plate, 5/16 inch thick and this had rounded rear corners to the superstructure. Seating arrangement was for 13 men, three in the driver's compartment, the remaining ten in two length-wise rows of five. A pedestal mount was fitted to the floor. This was the main type supplied to the British Army. The pilot model of this series was the M3E2. Total production of the M5 was 4,625 vehicles.

Brief details: Weight, 20,500 lb (gross); Crew, 13; Armour, 5/16 inch all round except windshield protective plate, 5/8 inch; Length, with roller, 20 ft 2 1/16 ins, with winch 20 ft 9 1/16 ins; Height, 7 ft 7 ins; Width, 7 ft 2 7/8 ins; Engine, International Red 450B 6 cylinder, 143 hp; Speed, 38 mph; Range, 125 miles; Ammunition stowage, Cal .30, 4,000 rds, Cal .45, 540 rds; Mine stowage, 24 (carried in side racks).

Half-Track Personnel Carrier, M5A1: This vehicle corresponded to the Half-Track Personnel Carrier M3A1, with seats for 13. It had a M49 ring mount and three fixed pintle sockets. Weight of this model was 21,500 lb (gross), 2,959 M5A1 vehicles were produced.

Half-Track Car, M5A2 (T31): This was a project to develop a vehicle to combine the essential features of the Half-Track M5 and M9 vehicles. Work was started in June 1943 at the International Harvester Company to modify three Half-Track Personnel Carriers M5 to provide stowage accommodation for all material to be carried in either the Half-Track M5 or M9 vehicles. These modified vehicles were designated T31 and were standardised in October 1943 as the Half-Track Car M5A2. This vehicle was intended for Lend-Lease supplies only, but never went into production. Accommodation for crews varied from 5 to 12 men; a ring mount M49 and three pintle sockets were fitted. Weight was 22,500 lb (gross).

Half-Track Car, M9A1: This was the International Harvester Company version of the M2A1, fitted with seats for ten men. It was provided with an M49 gun ring mount for a cal .50 machine gun and three fixed pintle sockets for a cal .30 machine gun. It was also equipped with a radio mast and rear door. This vehicle was developed as the M9, but the designation was changed to M9A1 before production began, by the fitting of the M49 ring mount. Some 3,433 vehicles were produced. These vehicles were the main type supplied to the British Army, where they were reworked to seat 13 men. Gross weight was 21,200 lb. Like the M5, this was distinguished from the M3 variants by the rounded rear corners to the superstructure, being of homogenous steel armour plate.

Half-Track Radio Car, T17: This was a special version for field communications carrying SCI 299 radio in a truck type body. It did not enter production.

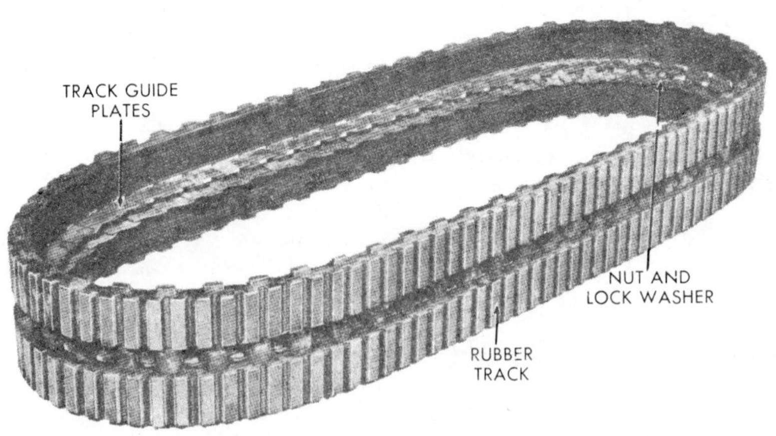

Track structure, standard for all vehicles.

CHAPTER THREE

MORTAR CARRIERS

AN IMPORTANT half-track type was the mortar carrier of which several different models were developed as direct derivatives from the personnel carriers.

Half-Track, 81 mm Mortar Carrier, M4: Based on the Half-Track Car, M2, this vehicle provided for the transport of the 81 mm Mortar with crew and ammunition. No provision was made for firing the mortar from the vehicle, save in extreme emergencies. Built by White, it was standardised in October 1940, and production was terminated in 1942 with a total of 572 built.

Half-Track, 81 mm Mortar Carrier, M4A1: This was generally similar to the Half-Track, 81 mm Mortar Carrier, M4, with modifications to permit the weapon to be placed in action with greater rapidity. The mortar could be traversed 600 mils (the M4, 130 mils). It could also be fired from the vehicle. Built by White, this vehicle was standardised in December 1942, a total of 600 vehicles being accepted.

Half-Track, 81 mm Mortar Carrier, M21 (T19): Deficiencies in the 81 mm Mortar Carrier M4 resulted in the development of a new mortar carrier based on the Half-Track Personnel Carrier, M3, with winch. This model, the T19, was modified to allow the mortar to fire from the vehicle to the front, with provision for removal for firing from the ground. Standardised in July 1943 as the M21, a total of 110 were built by White. A pedestal mount was provided for a cal .50 machine gun and a two-way radio was carried. Crew was six men and weight 18,500 lb (gross). All other details were as for Half-Track Personnel Carrier, M3.

4.2 inch Mortar Carrier, T21: Development of this weapon was begun in December 1942, to provide for installation of the standard 4.2 inch Chemical Mortar on the Half-Track Personnel Carrier, M3. Similar to the 81 mm Mortar Carrier, M4, the mortar was mounted to fire to the rear. A pilot model of the T21 was built and sent for trials, the results of which were satisfactory except for certain weaknesses in the mortar base installation. A M49 gun mount was fitted over the co-driver's seat, for a cal .50 machine gun.

4.2 inch Mortar Carrier, T21E1: After the testing of the T21, the military characteristics were revised to include the 4.2 inch mortar firing to the front of the vehicle and with certain changes in the stowage and machine gun mounts. A pilot model incorporating these changes was tested. The project was later dropped in

favour of mounting the 4.2 inch mortar on a full track vehicle. A pedestal mount
was fitted at the rear for a cal .50 machine gun.

Weight was 20,000 lb (gross) and crew five. Other details as for Half-Track
Personnel Carrier M3.

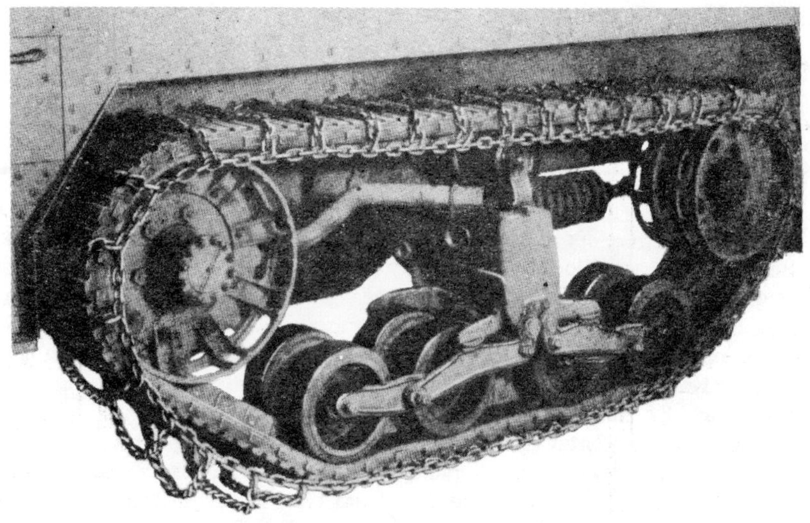

Track chain (used on ice or mud) was supplied to each vehicle.

CHAPTER FOUR

MULTIPLE GUN MOTOR CARRIAGES

THOUGH THE ORIGINAL purpose of the half-track vehicle had been to provide a means of transportation for personnel and cargo over soft and rough terrain, this role had been broadened considerably through the adoption of the half-track as a combat vehicle by the Armored Forces Command. Several thousand carriers were in service at the outbreak of the war, and lack of mobile gun carriages caused the Armored Force to consider the use of the half-track as an SP mount. While development work was under way for a full track tank destroyer, certain stop-gap weapons were developed. Of the three vehicles in this category, two mounted the 75 mm gun (T12) or 75 mm howitzer (T30) and the third used the 105 mm howitzer (T19). Despite their expedient nature, these weapons were highly successful. The T12/M3, an adaptation of the American version of the French 75 mm gun with the M3 half-track vehicle, was rushed to the Philippines in the autumn of 1941 where it performed excellent service. It later took part in the North African Campaign.

The use of dive-bombing and strafing tactics in Europe against troops and vehicles in 1939 and early 1940 made necessary the development and production of mobile anti-aircraft vehicles for the protection of motorised convoys. Though experiments with multiple machine gun mounts on trucks for anti-aircraft work had been carried out during 1929-1930, these had been discontinued and no further development of this type of weapon was made until 1940. The development programme for multiple gun motor carriages, weapons for the defence of troops and columns against aircraft, resulted in the idea of aircraft power-driven turrets being mounted on half-track vehicles. Standardisation of Multiple Gun Motor Carriages, M13 and M14, followed in 1942. These vehicles mounted two calibre .50 machine guns, and were succeeded, later in 1942, by the M16 and M17, carrying four calibre .50 machine guns. Development of a vehicle mounting a 37 mm gun with two calibre .50 machine guns was begun in 1941. This was standardised, as the M15, which as a stop-gap weapon proved successful as a defence against aircraft at low and medium heights and was produced in volume. The effectiveness of this weapon was proven in Tunisia during 1942, when over a three month period, vehicles of this type accounted for some 78 confirmed German planes, and probably shot down 20 others. Subsequently, development of vehicles combining the 40 mm gun and two calibre .50 machine guns was dropped in favour of vehicles armed solely with the more powerful gun. Experiments and development work with the M2 and M3 half-track vehicles as mobile SP mounts continued through 1943-44.

Multiple Gun Motor Carriage, T1E1: This featured twin calibre .50 machine guns in a Bendix power-operated turret, mounted on a M2 half-track car. Project was dropped with the standardisation of the Maxson turret.

Multiple Gun Motor Carriage, T1E2: This was an alternative design featuring a Maxson turret with twin calibre .50 machine guns on an elevating mechanism which in turn was mounted on a turntable capable of 360° at 74° per second. The mount could be elevated at 90° and depressed to 11.5°. Tested on a M2 half-track car, it proved better than the Bendix turret mount on the T1E1.

Multiple Gun Motor Carriage, T1E4: The Maxson turret with minor modifications was standardised as the Twin Cal .50 machine gun mount M33. For production the mount was placed on the M3 Personnel Carrier, a longer vehicle which provided more room for personnel, ammunition, and stowage. Designated T1E4, this vehicle was standardised as the Multiple Gun Motor Carriage M13 in July 1942.

Multiple Gun Motor Carriage, M13: This vehicle had an electrically operated gun mount M33 and carried its own battery charging unit. The turret had two calibre .50 machine guns, M2, HB with Edgewater adapter, and turned a full 360 degrees. There was no gun rail or pedestal mount or rear door on this model. There were hinged panels on the upper sides and rear to permit firing at 10° elevation. The fuel tanks were mounted just to the rear of the driver's compartment on each side of the body. The crew consisted of a gunner, two loaders, a driver and the commander. Each gun fired 400 to 500 rounds per minute, and had a maximum range of 7,200 yards. A $\frac{1}{4}$ inch front armour shield was provided for the protection of the gunner. These vehicles were manufactured by the Autocar Co, the Diamond T Motor Co, and the White Motor Co.

Multiple Gun Motor Carriage, M14: To speed production, Twin Cal .50 Machine Gun Mount, M33 was mounted on Half-Track Personnel Carrier, M5. The military characteristics except for slight changes were similar to that of the M13, and standardisation of the M14 was concurrent with that of the M13. Built by the International Harvester Co, 1,600 were supplied to the British Army who removed the guns and converted them into trucks, APCs and command vehicles. The British found less need for AA vehicles in the field, but conversely they were short of APCs, so conversion of the M14, unwanted in their intended role, was a convenient expedient.

Multiple Gun Motor Carriage, T1E3: This designation was applied to a Half-Track, M2, fitted with an experimental aircraft electro-dynamic power-operated turret designed by the Ordnance Section, Wright Field, for comparison with the Bendix turret on the T1E1, and the Maxson turret on the T1E2. It was not adopted.

Multiple Gun Motor Carriage, T28: This weapon consisted of the top portion of the 37 mm gun carriage, M3E1 mounting a 37 mm gun and two calibre .50 machine guns, mounted on Half-Track, M2. Tests proved satisfactory, but it was however recommended that the larger Half-Track Personnel Carrier, M3 be used. The project was closed with the reduced requirement for AA vehicles.

Multiple Gun Motor Carriage, T28E1: The making of 80 improvised 37 mm, self-propelled gun mounts for a special mission was directed by Headquarters, Services of Supply, in June 1942, so the project T28 was re-opened, using the Half-Track Personnel Carrier, M3. This vehicle was designated Multiple Gun Motor Carriage, T28E1. As the result of trials made with this vehicle, various modifications were made and the modified vehicle was put into production as the Multiple Gun Motor Carriage, M15.

Multiple Gun Motor Carriage, M15: 680 of these vehicles were built by the Autocar Co to provide an improved AA capability for the armoured formations, since the M13 and M14 gun motor carriages were not producing sufficient results. The M15 consisted of a fully automatic 37 mm gun and two cal .50 Browning machine guns mounted on an integral unit with M6 sighting system, designated Combination Gun Mount, M42. The mount was manually operated and had an elevation from 0° to 85° and a traverse of 360°. In the case of the first few vehicles of this type the weapons and crew were exposed, the only protection being around the driver's compartment. Later the weapons system was mounted in an armoured box at the rear of the chassis. The gun was designed to perform a dual role and could engage targets requiring a high elevation, like aircraft, or ground targets. The 37 mm gun had a sustained rate of fire of 40 rounds a minute, and the cal .50 machine guns, a rate of 500 rounds a minute. The HE shell fired from the 37 mm gun had a maximum range, vertical, of about 6,200 yards, and horizontal of about 8,875 yards. The maximum range of the cal .50 guns was about 7,200 yards. The cal .50 MGs were above the 37 mm gun in the combination mount.

Brief details: Weight, 20,000 lb (gross); Crew, 7; Armour, as for M3; Gun Shield, ¼ inch; Length, 20 ft 2 ½ inches; Height, 8 ft; Width, 6 ½ ft; Engine, White Model 160AX, 6 cylinder; Speed, 45 mph; Range, 200 miles; Ammunition Stowage, 37 mm, 240 rounds, cal .50, 3,400 rounds.

Multiple Gun Motor Carriage, M15A1: Built by Autocar, and standardised in August 1943, this was similar to the M15, but embodied several improvements. Combination Gun Mount, M54 was used, which consisted of the top carriage of the 37 mm Gun Carriage, M3A1 mounting a 37 mm gun, two cal .50 Browning machine guns and sighting system, M15. Interference between the guns and other equipment was eliminated at several points. A platform was provided for a loader, for the 37 mm gun and for the rate setter. The ammunition chests were separated to provide sufficient room for him to stand. The rate setter's seat was raised to facilitate operation of the sight. A rail was provided in the rear of the mount for aid of the gun crew in getting on the mount. The 37 mm gun was above the cal .50 MGs in the combination mount.

Multiple Gun Motor Carriage, T37 and T37E1: This was a project to mount four calibre .50 machine guns on a half-track vehicle. Two prototypes were developed. Designation T37 was applied to the Half-Track Personnel Carrier, M3, carrying Calibre .50 Machine Gun Mount, T60, in which the guns were mounted in square. The designation T37E1 was applied to the same vehicle mounting Calibre .50 Machine Gun Mount, T60E1, in which the guns were mounted in horizontal line.

On both vehicles the gun mount and crew were protected by a circular shield of $\frac{1}{2}$ inch plate, open at the top. As it was judged that the Multiple Gun Motor Carriages, M13, M15 and M16, developed later than the T37 and T37E1, were superior, this project was terminated.

Multiple Gun Motor Carriage, T58: Projected in April 1942, this was a development of a multiple machine gun mount to be basically like the M33 gun mount used on the M13 and M14, but mounting four guns instead of two. A pilot mount was tested on a Half-Track, M2 chassis. This was later changed to a Half-Track Personnel Carrier, M3, and this vehicle was designated Multiple Gun Motor Carriage, T58. As service tests of the gun mount proved satisfactory, the mount was standardised as Multiple Calibre .50 Machine Gun Mount, M45, and it was planned to replace the M33 gun mount in production as soon as possible. In December 1942, the M45 gun mount on the Half-Track Personnel Carrier, M3 was standardised as Multiple Gun Motor Carriage, M16.

Multiple Gun Motor Carriage, M16: 729 of these vehicles were built by White, and they consisted of four cal .50 Machine Guns, M2, HB(TT), in a Multiple Mount, M45, mounted on a Half-Track Personnel Carrier, M3. The mount, known as the Maxson turret, was essentially the same as that used on the Multiple Gun Motor Carriage, M13, which it replaced in production, but was modified to permit the use of four cal .50 guns instead of two. Each gun could fire 400 to 500 rounds per minute, and had a maximum range of 7,200 yards. The turret could be elevated from -10° to +90°, and had a traverse of 360° at a maximum speed of 60° per second. The gunner sat in a 45° reclining position on a fabric seat adjustable to his height. The crew consisted of five men, the driver and commander, two loaders, and a gunner, who was protected from the front against small arms fire by a shield of armour plate. The sides and rear of the vehicle could be folded down when the guns were in use. Two stowage boxes were provided at the rear of the vehicle.

Brief details: Weight, 18,000 lb (gross); Crew, 5; Armour, as for M3; Length, 21 ft 4 inches; Height, 7 ft 8 inches; Width, 7 ft 1 inch; Engine, White 160AX 6 cylinder, 45 mph; Range, 200 miles; Ammunition stowage, 5,000 rounds, cal .50.

Multiple Gun Motor Carriage, M17: Standardised at the same time as the M16, this was the M45 mount on the Half-Track Personnel Carrier, M5, built by International Harvester Co. It was similar to the Multiple Gun Motor Carriage, M16, except for the variations in the basic vehicles. 1,000 were built to termination of contract in 1944.

Multiple Gun Motor Carriage, T10: With the development of the Multiple Gun Motor Carriage, T1, the use of either calibre .50 or 20 mm guns had been contemplated. As the calibre .50 gun mount had been developed with the T1 series, the development of a vehicle mounting twin 20 mm guns was authorised in July 1941. Guns considered were the Oerlikon, the 20 mm Automatic Gun Mk IV, the Hispano-Suiza, and the 20 mm Automatic guns, AN-M1 and M2 mounted in a power-operated aircraft type turret. As constructed, this equipment consisted of twin 20 mm Oerlikons mounted in a Maxson turret carried on Half-Track M3.

Twin 20 mm Gun Motor Carriage, T10E1: This consisted of an improved gun mount, the T17E1 mounted on a modified Multiple Gun Motor Carriage M16.

Gun, Self Propelled, Half-Track M16A1 and M16A2: This was the designation given to refurbished M16s supplied by the US to friendly states under MDAP in the 1950s. For inventory purposes they were shown as US Ordnance items though were not actually used by the US Army.

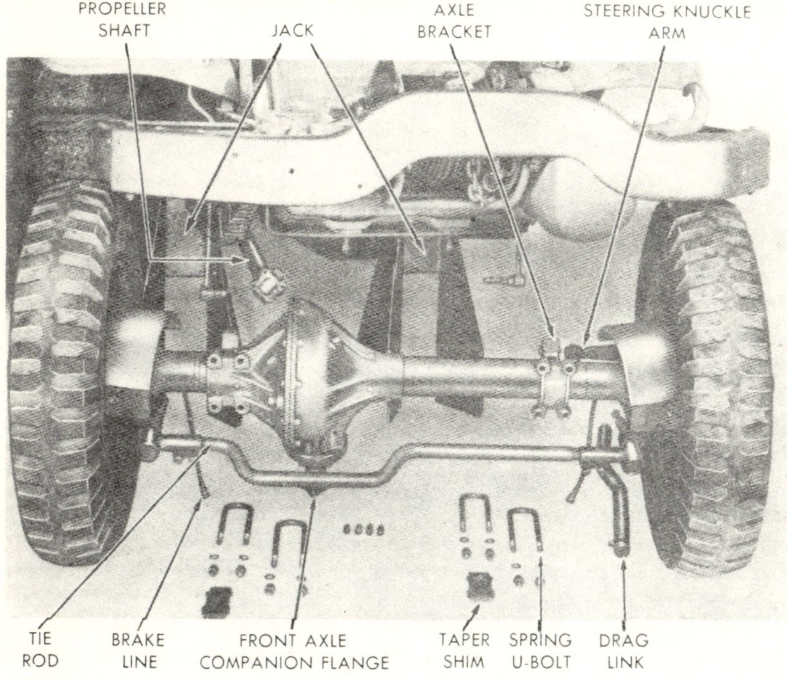

Front axle dis-assembled.

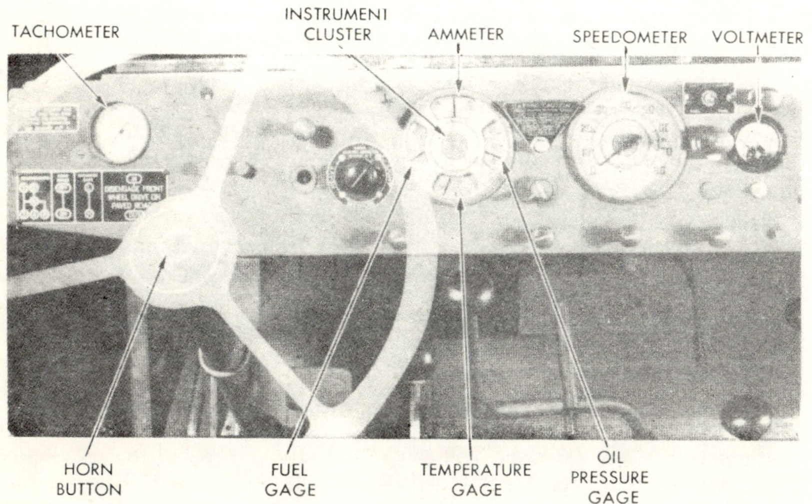

Instrument panel, White/Autocar/Diamond T vehicles.

CHAPTER FIVE

GUN MOTOR CARRIAGES

THE M3 SERIES also provided a basis for a whole range of expedient 'stop gap' designs of gun and howitzer self-propelled (ie, motor) carriages. These are described here.

40 mm Gun Motor Carriages, T1: Development of this weapon was begun in May 1941. It was intended to provide anti-aircraft protection for combat units. Gun, director, and power plant were to be mounted on the same chassis. The vehicle chosen was the Half-Track Chassis, T3, an experimental vehicle designed by the Mack Manufacturing Corporation. Mounted on this vehicle was a 40 mm Bofors gun, a Kerrison Director, and power plant. As the chassis proved unsuitable, the project was ended. On this chassis the engine was at the rear and the tracks were made up with standard components from the medium tank M3 series. The design was not related in any way to the standard half-track series, and the chassis is described later.

40 mm Gun Motor Carriages, T54 and T54E1: The T54, mounting the 40 mm gun, M1, on Half-Track Personnel Carrier M3 chassis was intended as an anti-aircraft weapon. Development was begun in June 1942, and one pilot model was completed and tested. A second pilot model was built with modifications to increase stability during firing, this vehicle was designated T54E1. Tests of the T54E1 showed that to stabilise the vehicle, both jacks and out-riggers would be required. The project was ended, the tests supplying engineering data for the T59 and T60 Gun Motor Carriages.

Multiple Gun Motor Carriage, T60 and T60E1: As a result of the trials of the 40 mm Gun Motor Carriage T54, modifications were proposed and a project was started to mount a 40 mm anti-aircraft gun with twin coaxial machine guns on a Half-Track M3. Two pilot models were built. The Multiple Gun Motor Carriage T60, with Combination Mount T65, mounting one 40 mm Automatic Gun M1 and two calibre .50 machine guns; the Multiple Gun Motor Carriage T60E1. this was a similar vehicle, but with modifications to the gun shields and stowage. This project was terminated in favour of later designs.

40 mm Gun Motor Carriages, T59 and T59E1: The purpose of this development was to mount a 40 mm power-operated anti-aircraft gun on a Half-Track M3, with the director and generator carried on an accompanying half-track, designated T59. This vehicle was fitted with quickly emplaced out-riggers and the means of blocking out the springs. As a result of the data received from the tests of the T54E1 carriage, the T59 was modified and provision made for mounting the Firing System T17. The modified vehicle was designated T59E1.

Half-Track Instrument Carrier, T18: This was the companion vehicle for the 40 mm Gun Carriage T59, based on the same type of vehicle, Half-Track M3, and carrying Director M5 and Generating Unit M5 with a transmission cable to supply power and control to the gun mount on the other vehicle.

40 mm Gun Motor Carriage, T68: Projected in 1943, this weapon consisted of two superimposed 40 mm guns with overhead equilibrators mounted on the chassis of Half-Track Personnel Carrier M3. One pilot model was built and tested; found unsuitable, the project was dropped.

57 mm Gun Motor Carriage, T48: This vehicle consisted of a 57 mm Gun M1, on 57 mm Gun Mount T5 fitted on a Half-Track Personnel Carrier M3. Its development was initiated by an Ordnance Committee action in April 1942, as an expedient mounting for the 57 mm (6 pdr) gun pending the development of a more suitable motor carriage for the weapon. It was originally expected that the vehicle would be manufactured to fill both United States and British requirements, but later developments resulted in production for the British only, the production programme being initiated in October 1942, with suitable British specifications. The 57 mm gun was mounted on the centre of the vehicle, immediately behind the front bulkhead, and fired to the front. A pivoted gunner's seat was provided, swinging independently of the gun. A travelling lock, with quick release, held the gun in place above the engine cover when not in use. The gun shield was of sloping, face-hardened armour plate, 5/8 inch thick at the front and $\frac{1}{4}$ inch at the sides and overhead. The 57 mm gun had an elevation from -5º to +15º and could be traversed 27$\frac{1}{2}$º right to 27$\frac{1}{2}$º left. Provision was made for carrying five British Lee-Enfield rifles. The vehicle was equipped with a British Wireless Set No 19; 962 of these vehicles were built by White, of which 680 were supplied to the British and the remainder were reconverted to M3A1 Carriers. These vehicles saw only limited use for by the time of their arrival in 1943 the 6 pdr was considered inadequate as an anti-tank gun and British armour doctrine made no provision for the use of half-tracks as SP guns. Many T48s were passed on to Russia and others were converted to troop carriers.

Brief details: Weight 19,000 lb (gross); Crew 5; Height 7 ft; Armour on Gun Shield (front) 5/8 inch, (sides and top) $\frac{1}{4}$ inch; Ammunition stowage (AP M70) 99 rounds. All other details of vehicle as for Half-Track M3.

75 mm Gun Motor Carriage, T12: In June 1941 a project was begun to mount a 75 mm gun on a Half-Track Personnel Carrier M3 for tests as an expedient tank destroyer, to be used pending design and production of a purpose-built self-propelled weapon intended primarily for anti-tank use. Use was made of the 75 mm Gun M1897A4 on a pedestal mount, firing forward, and protected by a gun shield. Designated 75 mm Gun Motor Carriage T12, tests were carried out with a pilot model, various types of gun shields being used. Design was standardised in October 1941 as the 75 mm Gun Motor Carriage M3. The 75 mm gun was from old ordnance stocks, the M1897A4 being used by the US Army on a field carriage before 1940.

75 mm Gun Motor Carriage, M3: This vehicle was the first standardised American self-propelled anti-tank weapon used in World War 2, providing high mobility for the 75 mm gun, it was put into production in time to aid in the rout of the German Army in North Africa. The 75 mm gun was carried on a Mount M3, a design adapted from the 75 mm Gun Carriage M2A3. It could be traversed 19° to the left and 21° to the right, and elevated from -10° to +29°. The shield traversed with the gun. The gun was loaded and operated from the crew compartment. Stowage space was provided for 59 rounds of ammunition and for a cal .30 rifle and four cal .30 carbines, the personal equipment of the crew. The fuel tanks were mounted at the rear, on each side of the vehicle. The body armour was the same as that of the Half-Track Personnel Carrier M3, including hinged protective shields for the windscreen and side doors. The vehicle was equipped with two-way radio. An APC projectile fired from the gun had a muzzle velocity of 2,000 feet per second, and could penetrate 3 inches of face-hardened armour at 1,000 yards. This vehicle was declared obsolete in September 1944. It was used in the Pacific Theatre and by the USMC as well as by the US Army.

Brief details: Weight 20,000 lb (gross); Crew 5; Armour on Gun Shield (front, sides and rear) $\frac{1}{4}$ inch; Ammunition stowage (75 mm HE/APC/AP) 59 rounds; Height 8 ft 2 5/8 inches. Vehicle details as for Half-Track M3.

In Tunisia, Sicily, and Italy, this particular vehicle was also used by the British in the HQ squadrons of some tank regiments to provide extra fire support. To the British it was known as the **75 mm SP, Autocar, M3.**

75 mm Gun Motor Carriage, M3A1: Due to a shortage of the 75 mm Gun Carriage M2A3, use was made of 75 mm Gun Carriage M2A2, from which was adapted the Gun Mount M5. It could be elevated from -6 $\frac{1}{2}$° to +29° and traversed 21° right and 21° left. In all other characteristics this equipment was similar to the M3 GMC.

75 mm Gun Motor Carriage, T73: This was a redesigned M3 GMC, mounting a 75 mm Gun M3 instead of the model M1897A4 gun. The 75 mm Gun M3 was the same model as that used in the Sherman tank.

75 mm Howitzer Motor Carriage, T30: Successful use of Half-Track Personnel Carrier M3 as a basic vehicle for mounting the 75 mm gun resulted in the experimental mounting of the 75 mm howitzer on the same vehicle. Designed as an expedient to provide a 75 mm howitzer on a self-propelled mount, the project was initiated in October 1941 and a contract for the manufacture of two pilot models was given to the Autocar Co in December 1941. The weapon, designated 75 mm Howitzer Motor Carriage T30, consisted of a 75 mm Howitzer M1A1, mounted on a Half-Track Personnel Carrier M3. The howitzer had elevations from -9° to +50° and a traverse of 22 $\frac{1}{2}$° right and 22 $\frac{1}{2}$° left. It fired a 14.6 pound projectile, with a muzzle velocity of 1,250 feet per second, and at an elevation of 13 $\frac{1}{2}$°, the howitzer had a maximum range of 9,610 yards.

The T30 had a rear door, and a modified Pedestal Mount M25 at the rear centre for mounting a Cal .50 Machine Gun, M2 HB, for anti-aircraft protection. There was no skate rail inside the vehicle body and the fuel tanks were fitted at the rear sides. Various designs of gunshields were constructed and tested at the Aberdeen Proving Ground. Subsequently, 500 of these vehicles were manufactured by the White Motor Co, though 188 of them were later re-converted to Half-Track Personnel Carrier M3 standard.

Brief details: Weight 19,500 lb; Crew 5; Ammunition stowage (75 mm) 60 rounds; Height 8 ft ¾ inch; Armour (windshield) ½ inch, (gunshield) 3/8 inch, (sides and rear) ¼ inch. Other details as for M3.

105 mm Howitzer Motor Carriage, T19: This weapon was designed as an expedient to provide a 105 mm howitzer on a self-propelled mount. The project was initiated in October 1941. Mounted on the Half-Track Personnel Carrier M3, the principal weapon was the 105 mm Howitzer M2A1 on 105 mm Howitzer Mount T2. With elevation from -5° to +35° and a traverse of 20° right and 20° left, it fired a HE shell with a muzzle velocity of 1,550 feet per second. A range of 11,700 yards was achieved with maximum elevation of the gun. The T19 had a rear door, and was fitted with a modified Pedestal Mount M25 for mounting a Cal .50 Machine Gun M2 HB for anti-aircraft protection. There was no skate rail fitted inside the vehicle and the fuel tanks were mounted at the rear sides. Various gunshields were fitted. The T19 was first used in North Africa and equipped the HQ companies of some tank battalions to give fire support. In 1943 they were replaced by the M8 Howitzer Motor Carriage which was developed as a specialised type for this role. Diamond T built a total of 324 T19s.

Brief details: Weight 20,000 lb (gross); Crew 6; Height 7 ft 8 inches; Armour (windshield) ½ inch, and (sides and rear) ¼ inch; Ammunition stowage 105 mm Howitzer, 8 rounds, and Cal .50, 300 rounds. All other details as for the basic M3 model.

105 mm Howitzer Motor Carriage T19E1: To provide superior protection for the gun crew, an armoured shield was designed that fitted over the mounting and extended each side. Only the pilot model was produced.

105 mm Howitzer Motor Carriage, T38: A short tube 105 mm Howitzer T7 was mounted on the Half-Track Personnel Carrier M3 and was tested. However, no further development was undertaken.

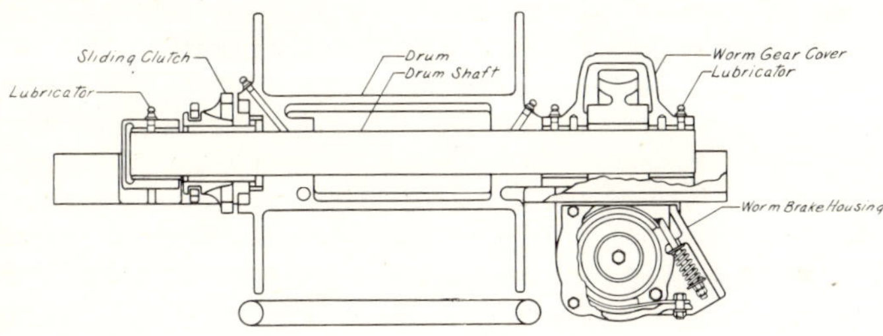

Section through winch from front. Winch was mounted between chassis frame side rails at front of vehicles so fitted. It was rated at 10,000 lb. and was driven by a propeller shaft from the power take-off on the transfer case.

CHAPTER SIX

HALF-TRACK TRUCKS

LASTLY COMES a group of vehicles which were initiated as replacements for the M3/M9 designs and their derivatives. These were the Half-Track Trucks, totally new designs. However, the US Army's decision to switch entirely to tracked vehicles for the armoured divisions led to a premature end for the development programme.

Half-Track Truck, T16: This was a project to develop a prime mover for light artillery weapons and to transport personnel, ammunition and miscellaneous cargo pertaining to the section. The first pilot was completed by Diamond T Motor Company in March 1943 and the second in June 1943. The project was discontinued due to the cancellation of the military requirement. A pedestal mount was fitted for a cal .50 MG.

Brief details: Weight, 30,010 lb (gross); Crew, 14; Armour $\frac{1}{4}$ inch; Length, 20 ft 7 3/8 ins; Height, 7 ft 10 ins; Width, 7 ft 10 ins; Engine, Hercules R.XLD, 6-cylinder, 174 hp; Speed, 35 mph; Range, 200 miles.

Half-Track Truck, T17: Developed to provide a prime mover and carrier for the artillery as an alternative design to the Half-Track Truck, T16. One pilot model was built by Autocar Company in June 1943, and one by the White Motor Company in August 1943. It was fitted with the M49 ring mount for the cal .50 MG. The project was discontinued due to lack of military requirements.

Brief details: Weight, 30,761 lb (gross): Crew, 14; Armour, $\frac{1}{4}$ inch (front, sides, rear); Length, 20 ft 4 $\frac{1}{4}$ ins; Height, 7 ft. 6 $\frac{1}{4}$ ins; Width, 8 ft 6 $\frac{1}{2}$ ins; Engine, White Model 24, 12 cylinder, 210 hp; Speed, 37 mph; Range, 150 miles.

Half-Track Truck, T19: Designed and developed as a second alternative to the Half-Track Truck, T16. Two pilot models were built by the Mack Manufacturing Corporation. The first pilot was completed in November 1942, the second in April 1943. Then the project was discontinued; 40 rounds of 105 mm howitzer were carried in this model.

Brief details: Weight, 28,800 lb (gross); Crew, 14; Armour, $\frac{1}{4}$ inch (front, sides, rear); Length, 20 ft 6 3/8 ins; Height, 7 ft 2 ins; Width, 8 ft 5 ins; Engine, Continental, Model R6572, 6 cylinder, 215 hp; Speed 37.7 mph; Range, 115 miles.

CHAPTER SEVEN

POST-WAR SERVICE

IN POST-WAR YEARS the half-tracks soldiered on, more widely used in fact than they had been during the war, despite the fact that all production of new vehicles actually ceased well before the end of World War 2. Hundreds of surplus-stored vehicles were disposed of by America to friendly nations and the NATO states. Mainly these were personnel carrier models, but the M16 and M17 Multiple Gun Motor Carriages were also in wide use. In fact the US half-tracks had a longer continuous service life than any other American vehicle of the war years, for even most of the original Jeeps were eventually replaced by later models. Not so the half-track, however. Well into the 1970s it was still in service with some NATO armies and over the years it has been standard equipment in Spain, France, Italy, Japan, Britain, the Philippines, Cambodia, and Greece, to mention just a short list of main users. British developed versions were a command vehicle, with hard top added, used mainly at brigade level until the early 1960s, and a REME recovery model with front-mounted jib and winch and workshop facilities in the back. Even in 1971 a few of these vehicles remained in British service, mainly because they had a higher vertical lift capability than the vehicles designed to replace them, ie, the repair and recovery version of the standard tracked carrier.

The major users of the American half-track in post-war years were, of course, the Israelis, for whom it became the standard armoured division vehicle used extensively by the mechanised infantry. Hundreds of half-tracks of various models were acquired from nations disposing of their unwanted vehicles and these were extensively rebuilt in Israel. In fact, Israel has a depot devoted exclusively to reconditioning half-tracks and it is believed that at one time they gave serious consideration to putting their own version of the design into production in Israel. Most Israeli half-tracks have a Browning machine gun added in the co-driver's position, and some have hard-tops added, mainly, it is believed, on command vehicles. Another Israeli variant has French SS-11 anti-tank missiles on launchers in the rear compartment. The American half-track vehicles thus look certain of staying in first-line service for some years to come, undoubtedly setting the record, already 30 years, for the longest-lived of all basic military designs to remain in such wide use.

U.S. ARMOURED HALF-TRACK VEHICLES

Original Nomenclature (1) (in M- and T- number order)	Year (2)	Basic Vehicle	Type/ Manufacturer (3)	Classification (4) 1943	1947	1953	1955	Crew
Car, Half-Track, M2	41	M.2	S(A, W)	S	LA	–	–	10
Car, Half-Track, M2 E1	41	M.2	S	–	–	–	–	10
Car, Half-Track, M2 E2	41	M.2	S	–	–	–	–	10
Car, Half-Track, M2 E3	41	M.2	S	–	–	–	–	10
Car, Half-Track, M2 E4	41	M.2	S	–	–	–	–	10
Car, Half-Track, M2 E5	41	M.2	S	–	–	–	–	10
Car, Half-Track, M2 E6	41	M.2	S	–	–	–	–	10
Car, Half Track, M2 A1	42	M.2	S(A, W)	S	LS	LS	LS	10
Carrier, Personnel, Half-Track, M3	41	M.3	S(A, D, W)	S	S	LS	LS	13
Carrier, Personnel, Half-Track, M3 E2	41	M.3	S	–	–	–	–	13
Carrier, Personnel, Half-Track, M3 A1	42	M.3	S(A, D, W)	S	LS	LS	LS	13
Car, Half-Track, M3 A2	42	M.3	S	–	–	–	–	13
Car, Half-Track, M3 A3	42	M.3	S	–	–	–	–	13
Car, Half-Track, M3 A4	42	M.3	S	–	–	–	–	13
Carriage, Motor, 75mm. Gun, M3	41	M.3	S(A)	S	–	–	–	5
Carriage, Motor, 75mm. Gun, M3 A1	41	M.3	S(A)	S	–	–	–	5
Carrier, 81mm. Mortar, Half-Track, M4	41	M.2	S(W)	SS	LS	LS	–	6
Carrier, 81mm. Mortar, Half-Track, M4 A1	41	M.2	S(W)	S	LS	LS	LS	6
Carrier, Personnel, Half-Track, M5	41	M.5	IHC	S	–	–	–	13
Carrier, Personnel, Half-Track M5 A1	41	M.5	IHC	S	–	–	–	13
Car Half-Track, M9	41	M.5	IHC	–	–	–	–	10
Car, Half-Track, M9 A1	42	M.5	IHC	SS	LS	–	–	10
Carriage, Motor, Multiple Gun, M13	42	M.3	S(W)	SS	–	–	–	5
Carriage, Motor, Multiple Gun, M14	42	M.5	IHC	SS	–	–	–	5
Carrier, Personnel, Half-Track, M14	43	M.14	IHC	–	–	–	–	10
Truck, 15 cwt., Half-Track, GS	43	M.14	IHC	–	–	–	–	2
Truck, 15 cwt., Half-Track, Command	43	M.14	IHC	–	–	–	–	2
Carriage, Motor, Combination Gun, M15	43	M.3	S(A)	LS	–	–	–	7
Carriage, Motor, Combination Gun, M15 A1	43	M.3	S(A)	S	LS	LS	LS	7
Carriage, Motor, Multiple Gun, M16	43	M.3	S(W)	S	LS	SS	SS	5
Gun, Self Propelled, Half-Track, M16 A1	PW	M.3	S	–	–	–	SS	5
Gun, Self Propelled, Half-Track, M16 A2	PW	M.3	S	–	–	–	SS	5
Carriage, Motor, Multiple Gun, M17	42	M.5	IHC	SS	–	–	–	5
Carrier, Mortar, 81mm., Half-Track, M21	42	M.3	S(W)	S	S	S	S	6
Carriage, Motor, Multiple Gun, T1 E1	41	M.2	S	–	–	–	–	5
Carriage, Motor, Multiple Gun, T1 E2	42	M.2	S	–	–	–	–	5
Carriage, Motor, Multiple Gun, T1 E3	42	M.2	S	–	–	–	–	5
Carriage, Motor, Multiple Gun, T1 E4	42	M.3	S	–	–	–	–	5
Carriage, Motor, Multiple Gun, T10	42	M.2	S	–	–	–	–	5
Carriage, Motor, Multiple Gun, T10 E1	43	M.3	S	–	–	–	–	5
Carriage, Motor, 75mm. Gun, T12	41	M.3	S(A)	–	–	–	–	5
Car, Half-Track, T16	42	M.2	S(A)	–	–	–	–	10
Carrier, Radio, Half-Track, T17	43	M.3	S	–	–	–	–	?
Carrier, Instrument, Half-Track, T18	43	M.3	S	–	–	–	–	?
Carriage, Motor, 105mm. Howitzer, T19	41	M.3	S(D)	–	–	–	–	6
Carrier, 81mm. Mortar, Half-Track, T19	41	M.2	S(D)	–	–	–	–	6
Carrier, 4.2 in. Mortar, Half-Track, T21	41	M.3	S	–	–	–	–	6
Carriage, Motor, Combination Gun, T28	42	M.3	S	–	–	–	–	7
Carriage, Motor, Combination Gun, T.23 E1	42	M.3	S	–	–	–	–	7
Car, Half-Track, T29	41	M.3	S	–	–	–	–	10
Carriage, Motor, 75mm. Howitzer, T30	42	M.3	S(W)	–	–	–	–	5
Car, Half-Track, T31	41	M.5	IHC	–	–	–	–	10
Carriage, Motor, Multiple Gun, T37	42	M.3	S	–	–	–	–	5
Carriage, Motor, Multiple Gun, T37 E1	42	M.3	S	–	–	–	–	5
Carriage, Motor, 105mm. Howitzer, T38	42	M.3	S	–	–	–	–	?
Carriage, Motor, 57mm. Gun, T48	42	M.3	S(D)	–	–	–	–	5
Carriage, Motor, 40mm. Gun, T54	42	M.3	S	–	–	–	–	?
Carriage, Motor, 40 mm. Gun, T54 E1	42	M.3	S	–	–	–	–	?
Carriage, Motor, Multiple Gun, T58	42	M.2/3	S	–	–	–	–	5
Carriage, Motor, 40mm. Gun, T59	43	M.3	S	–	–	–	–	?
Carriage, Motor, 40mm. Gun, T59 E1	43	M.3	S	–	–	–	–	?
Carriage, Motor, Combination Gun, T60	43	M.3	S	–	–	–	–	?
Carriage, Motor, Combination Gun, T60	43	M.3	S	–	–	–	–	?
Carriage, Motor, Multiple Gun, T61 E1	43	M.2	S	–	–	–	–	5
Carriage, Motor, Multiple Gun, T68	43	M.3	S	–	–	–	–	5
Carriage, Motor, 75mm. Gun, T73	43	M.3	S	–	–	–	–	5

Key to Column Headings:
(1) DESIGNATION: M = Standardised; T = Experimental; A = Standardised Modification; E = Experimental Modification.
(2) YEAR: Year (sometimes approximate) when vehicle or version was first produced. PW = post-war.
(3) TYPE/MANUFACTURER: S = Standardised type chassis (Where known; A = Autocar; D = Diamond T; W = White); IHC = International Harvester Co.

Body Type spans the three hull columns ('short hull', 'long hull', no hull (5)).

with winch	with roller	Machine Gun Ring Mount	'short hull'	'long hull'	no hull (5)	Remarks
●	●	–	●	–	–	originally T7.
●	●	–	●	–	–	armoured top.
●	●	–	●	–	–	scout car; steel tracks; IHC components.
●	●	–	●	–	–	modified M2 E2.
●	●	–	●	–	–	Hercules diesel engine.
●	●	–	●	–	–	IHC components; became M9; steel tracks.
●	●	●	●	–	–	unarmoured ring mount; became M2 A1.
●	●	●	●	–	–	armoured ring mount.
●	●	–	–	●	–	originally T14 Scout Car.
●	●	–	–	●	–	IHC components; became M5
●	●	●	–	●	–	armoured ring mount.
●	●	●	–	●	–	enlarged ring mount.
●	●	●	–	●	–	modified M3 A2
●	●	●	–	●	–	enlarged ring mount.
–	●	–	–	●	–	tank destroyer; originally T12.
–	●	–	–	●	–	improved M3 using different gun mount (M5).
●	●	–	●	–	–	originally mortar carrier.
●	●	–	●	–	–	improved version of M4.
●	●	–	–	●	–	IHC version of M3; used mainly by British.
●	●	●	–	●	–	M5 with armoured ring mount.
●	●	–	–	●	–	IHC version of M2; did not enter production.
●	●	●	–	●	–	M9 with armoured ring mount; used by British.
●	●	–	–	●	–	based on M3 carriage; originally T1 E4 (see there).
●	–	–	–	●	–	similar M13; many modified (see below).
●	–	–	–	●	–	M14 modified for personnel (APC); British Army.
●	–	–	–	●	–	M14 modified for GS cargo and other roles; Canadian and British Army.
●	–	–	–	●	–	M14 modified for Command role; British.
–	●	–	–	–	●	37mm. AA gun and 2.50 cal. machine guns (all 3 guns synchronised).
–	●	–	–	–	●	improved M15;
●	–	–	–	●	–	4.50 cal. machine guns; originally T58 (on M2); known as "Wipper"; hinged-top side panels.
●	●	–	–	●	–	armoured shields; full-height body sides.
●	●	–	–	●	–	modified M16 A1.
●	–	–	–	●	–	4.50 cal. machine guns; IHC version of M16.
●	–	–	–	●	–	later: Carrier, 81mm. Mortar, Half-Track, M21.
–	●	–	–	–	●	2.50 cal. machine guns; Bendix aircraft type turret; project dropped.
–	●	–	–	–	●	as T1 E1 but Maxson turret.
–	●	–	–	–	●	as T1 E1 but Wright Field turret.
–	●	–	–	●	–	2.50 cal. Machine guns; power-operated turret; became M13
–	●	–	–	–	●	2.20mm. Oerlikons in Maxson turret.
●	–	–	–	●	–	as T10 but mounted on M16 carriage.
–	●	–	–	●	–	75mm. gun; various gun shields; became M3.
–	●	–	●	–	–	overhead armour; extended track bogies.
–	–	–	–	–	–	SC1 299 radio set in unarmoured truck body.
–	●	–	–	●	–	built-up hull with square cupola; companion vehicle to T59 (Bofors).
–	●	–	–	●	–	various protecting shields; used in North Africa.
●	●	–	●	–	–	modified Car M2; became M4.
●	–	–	–	●	–	chemical mortar.
–	●	–	–	–	●	37mm. gun and 2.50 cal. machine guns in rotating mount.
–	●	–	–	–	●	improved T28; became M15.
●	●	●	–	●	–	projected universal body.
–	●	–	–	●	–	Pack howitzer, with or without shield; 500 built.
●	●	●	–	●	–	projected universal body.
–	●	–	–	●	–	4.50 cal. machine guns in circular open-top turret.
–	●	–	–	●	–	modified T37; parallel .50 cal. machine guns.
–	●	–	–	●	–	short-tube howitzer T7; project suspended.
●	●	–	–	●	–	built for British, to their specification.
–	●	–	–	●	–	Bofors AA gun.
–	●	–	–	●	–	T54 with open circular turret, shield, and jacks (outriggers).
●	–	–	–	●	–	4.50 cal. machine guns; became M16/M17 (IHC).
–	●	–	–	●	–	Bofors AA gun; companion to T18.
–	●	–	–	●	–	modified hull and various other modifications.
–	●	–	–	●	–	40mm. gun and 2.50 cal. machine guns; modified T54 E1.
–	●	–	–	●	–	as T60 but redesigned shields and re-arrangement of stowage.
–	●	–	–	●	–	4.50 cal. machine guns; similar to T58.
–	●	–	–	–	–	twin Bofors with equilibrator; mock-up body.
–	●	–	–	●	–	75mm. M3 A/T gun.

(4) CLASSIFICATION: S = Standard; SS = Substitute Standard; LS = Limited Standard; – = Not classified, or obsolete (source; TM9-2800).

(5) Armoured open-top cab and open-sided rear body.

Half-Track Specifications – Vehicles built by Autocar/Diamond T/White

	M2	M2A1	M3	M3A1	M3A2
Crew	10	10	13	13	5 to 12
Characteristics					
Weight (gross)	19,800lb.	19,600lb.	20,000lb.	20,500lb.	21,200lb.
Length – with roller	19ft., $6^3/_4$in.	19ft., $6^3/_4$in.	20ft., $3^1/_2$in.	20ft., $3^1/_2$in.	20ft., $3^1/_2$in.
Length – with winch	20ft., 1 5/8in.	20ft., 1 5/8in.	20ft., 9 5/8in.	20ft., 9 5/8in.	20ft., 9 5/8in.
Width – without mine racks	6ft., $5^1/_4$in.	6ft., $5^1/_4$in.	6ft., $5^1/_4$in.	6ft., $5^1/_4$in.	6ft., $5^1/_4$in.
Width – with mine racks	7ft., $3^1/_2$in.	7ft., $3^1/_2$in.	7ft., $3^1/_2$in.	7ft., $3^1/_2$in.	7ft., $3^1/_2$in.
Height – overall	7ft., 5in.	8ft., 10in.	7ft., 5in.	8ft., 10in.	8ft., 10in.
Ground clearance	11 3/16in.	11 3/16in.	11 3/16in.	11 3/16in.	11 3/16in.
Tread – front	$64^1/_2$in.	$64^1/_2$in.	$64^1/_2$in.	$64^1/_2$in.	$64^1/_2$in.
Tread – rear	63 13/16in.	63 13/16in.	63 13/16in.	63 13/16in.	63 13/16in.
Wheelbase	$135^1/_2$in.	$135^1/_2$in.	$135^1/_2$in.	$135^1/_2$in.	$135^1/_2$in.
Ground contact	$46^3/_4$in.	$46^3/_4$in.	$46^3/_4$in.	$46^3/_4$in.	$46^3/_4$in.
Tyre size (combat, 12-ply)	8.25×20	8.25×20	8.25×20	8.25×20	8.25×20
Armament					
Cal. .50 Machine Gun M2, HB (flexible)	1	1		1	1
Cal. .30 Browning Machine Gun M1919A4 (flexible)	1	1	1	1	1
Pedestal Mount M25			1		
Ring Mount M49 for cal. .30 or cal. .50 Machine Gun		1		1	
Carriage assembly		1		1	
Cradle assemblies		2	1	2	
Cal. .50 Tripod Mount M3	1	1		1	
Cal. .30 Tripod Mount M2	1	1	1	1	1
Machine Gun Mounts M35	2				
Provision for:					
Rocket Launcher, AT, 2.36-in., M9 or M1A1					1
Cal. .45 Sub-Machine Gun M3 or M1928A1	1	1	1	1	1
Cal. .30 Rifles M1 or Carbines M1			12	12	12
Ammunition, Stowage					
Cal. .50	700 rounds	700 rounds	700 rounds	700 rounds	330 rounds
Cal. .30	7,750 rounds	7,750 rounds	4,000 rounds	7.750 rounds	2,000 rounds
Cal. .45	540 rounds	540 rounds	540 rounds	540 rounds	180 rounds
Rockets, Grenade, AT, 2.36-in., M6					6
Grenades, Hand (Fragmentation, Mk.II: Smoke, WP, M15, Smoke, Coloured, M6 or M18)	10	10	22	22	24
Mines, AT, H.E., w/Fuze M1	14	14	24	24	24

Armour – Front 1/4in.
   Sides and rear 1/4in., F.H.
   Windshield protective plate 1/2in.

Performance
   Maximum speed on level 40 m.p.h.
   Maximum grade ability 60%
   Vertical obstacle ability 12in.
   Fording depth (slowest forward speed) 32in.
   Turning radius 30ft.
   Fuel capacity 60 gal.
   Cruising range (approx.) 175 miles

Vision
   Driver   Slits in windshield and wingshield

Communications
   Radio   SCR-193 or 506, and 508 and 593;
   284 and 508 and 593; 193 or 506,
   and 508 or 528 or 510 or 608 or 610
   or 628. (Or any individual set)

Battery 12 volts

Fire Protection and Decontamination
   Fire Extinguisher, CO₂-4lb. (hand) 1
   Decontaminating Apparatus M2, 1 1/2qt. 3

Engine, Make and model White 160AX
   Type In-Line, "L"
   No. of cylinders 6
   Cycle 4
   Fuel (petrol) 80 octane
   Bore and stroke 4 × 5 1/8in.
   Displacement 386 cu. in.
   Compression 6.3:1
   Net hp 128 at 2,800 r.p.m.
   Max. torque 300 lb.-ft. at 1,200 r.p.m.
   Length 52 1/4in.
   Width 26in.
   Height 37in.
   Ignition Battery
   Weight, dry 1,015lb.
   Weight, installed 1,207lb.

Transmission, Gear ratios
   First speed 4.92:1
   Second speed 2.60:1
   Third speed 1.74:1
   Fourth speed 1.00:1
   Reverse 4.37:1

Transfer Case
   Gear ratios 1.00:1, 2.48:1

Differential, Track Drive, Gear ratiO 4.444:1
   Ring gear, No. of teeth 40
   Pinion, No. of teeth 9
Differential, Front Axle, Gear ratio 6.8:1
   Ring gear, No. of teeth 34
   Pinion, No. of teeth 5
   Steering ratio 23.4; 19.5; 23.4:1
Final Drive
   Sprocket, No. of teeth 18
   Pitch diameter 22.918 in.
Suspension, Track, Type Volute spring
   Wheel or tyre size 12 × 4 1/8 dual
Suspension, Front
   Type (longitudinal leaf) Semi-elliptic
   Wheel or tyre size 8.25 × 20
   Wheel construction Ventilated disc
Idler, Wheel size 12 1/2 × 9 3/8
Track, Type Endless band
   Width 12in.
   Pitch 4in
Master Clutch, Type Dry single plate
Radiator, Type Fin and tube
   Capacity of system 26qt.
Brakes, Type Internal expanding
   Operation Hydraulic
Brakes, Parking, Type Disc

Half-Track Specifications – Vehicles built by International Harvester Co.

Characteristics
   Weight (gross)-M9A1 21,200lb.
   M5 20,500lb.
   M5A1 21,500lb.
   M5A2 22,500lb.
   Length – with roller 20ft., 2 3/16in.
   Length – with winch 20ft., 9 1/16in.
   Width – over mine racks 7ft., 2 7/8in.
   Height – over bows 7ft., 7in.
   Top of A.A. gun (M49 Mount) 9ft.
   Ground clearance 11 3/16in.
   Tread – front 66 1/2in.
   Tread – rear 63 13/16in.
   Wheelbase 135 1/2in.
   Tyre size 9.00 × 20 (combat)

Armour – Front, sides, and rear 5/16in. homo.
   Floor 5/16in.
   Windshield protective plate 5/8in.

Performance
   Maximum speed on level 38 m.p.h.
   Maximum grade ability 60%
   Vertical obstacle ability 12in.
   Fording depth 32in.
   Angle of approach – with roller 40°
      with winch 36°
   Angle of departure 32°
   Fuel capacity 60 gal.
   Cruising range (approx.) 125 miles
   Normal towed load 4,500 lb.

Engine, Make International
   Model RED 450B
   Type In-line, L.C.
   Number of cylinders 6
   Cycle 4
   Fuel (petrol) 80 octane
   Max. governed speed 2,700 r.p.m.
   Net hp 143 at 2,700 r.p.m.
   Max. torque 348 lb.-ft. at 800 r.p.m.

Radiator, Capacity 31 qt.

Other characteristics were the same as for corresponding models in Half-Track M2 and M3 series.

Half-Track Personnel Carrier M3 with all stowage compartments open to show tools and accessories.

Ordnance Department Half-Track Diagrams

The drawings on the following pages are reproduced from the official US Ordnance Department control diagrams for major production models and are representative for all models. The originals were dye-line drawings scaled at 1 ½ inches to 1 foot. Due to the big reduction in what were originally, in any case, old drawings, there is an inevitable loss of quality. All are reproduced to a common size (the largest possible on the page) and in some cases this means that edges or captions may be slightly clipped. In some instances they were missing from the originals. The captions provided are those given on the original sheets.

Note on Nomenclature

Despite standardisation of designs and equipment there was some variation in official nomenclature of half-track vehicles. In the main text we have used a compromise system which reflects common (and usually official) descriptions. The tabular summary on the previous pages gives designations as listed in the official publication TM9-2800 just after World War 2. It can be seen that this sometimes varies slightly from official designations as given on the US Ordnance Department diagrams shown in the next section.

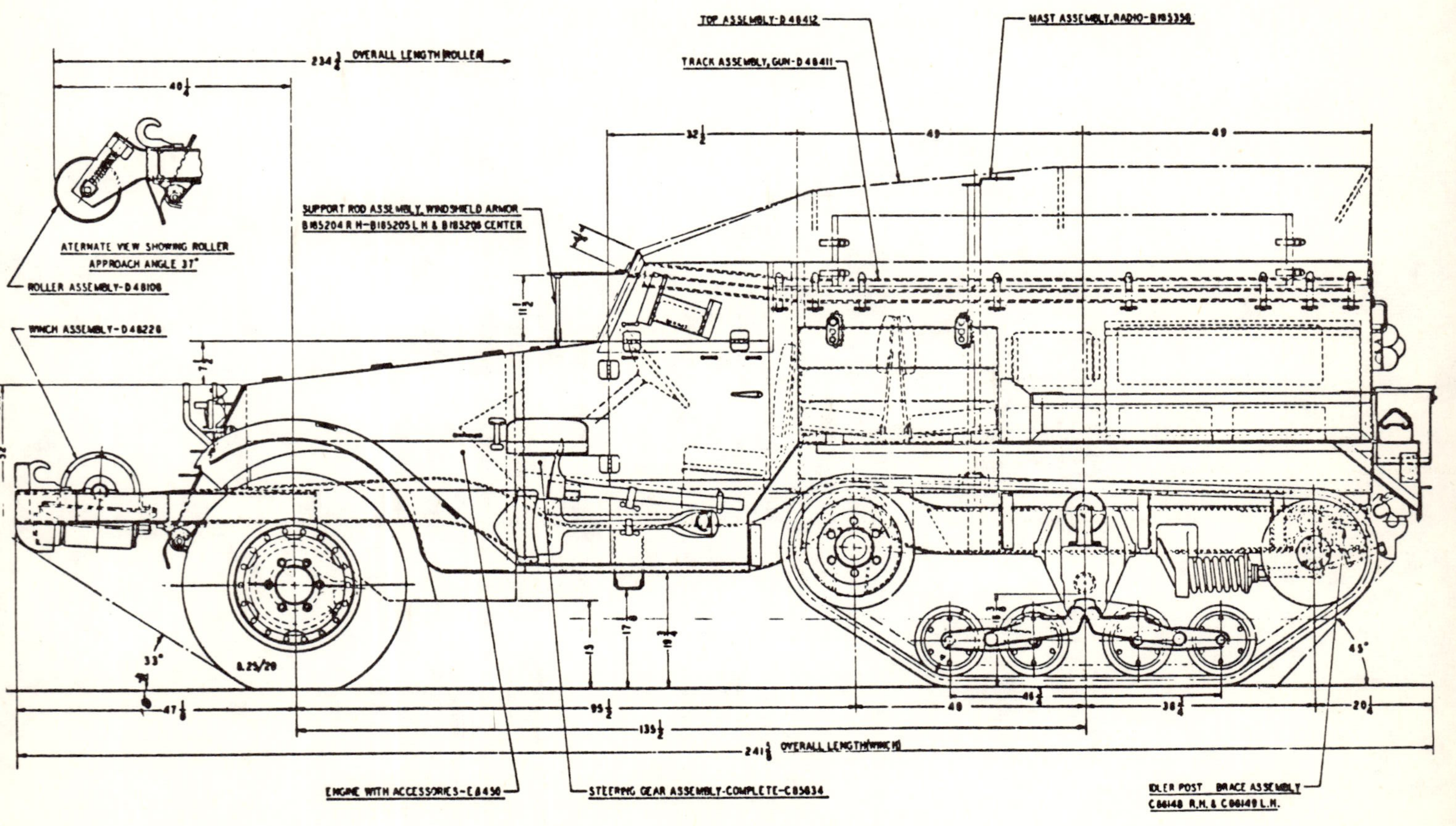

Car, Half-Track, M2 (left side)

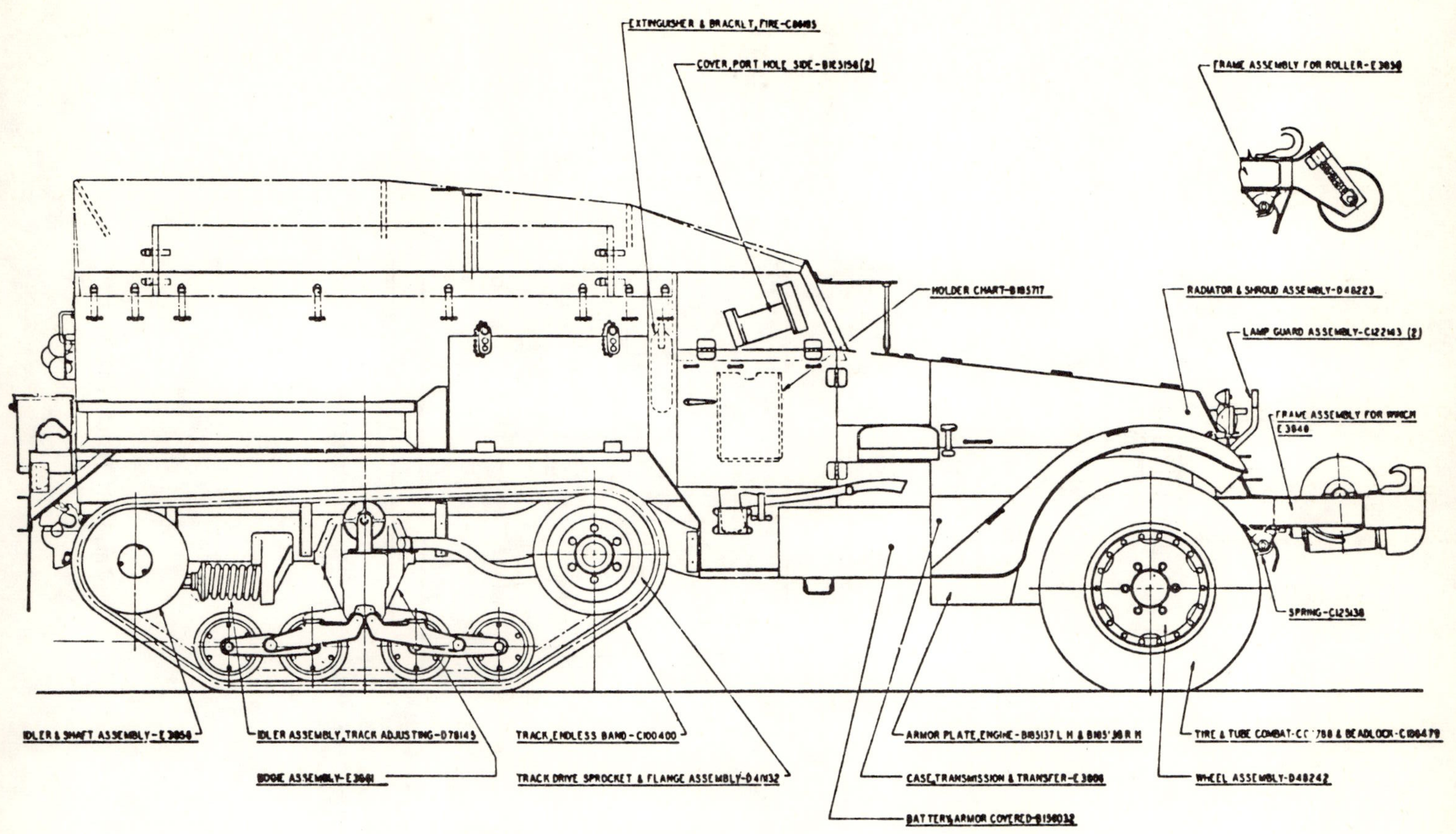

Car, Half-Track, M2 (right side)

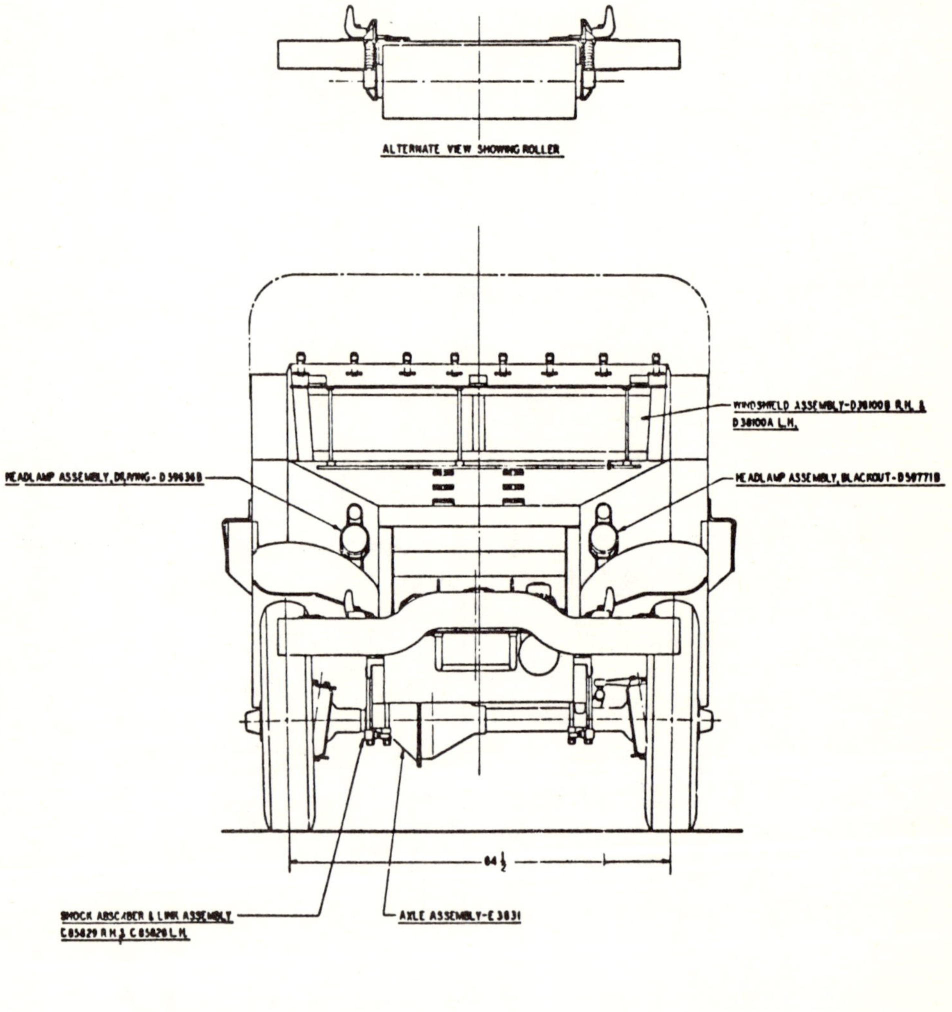

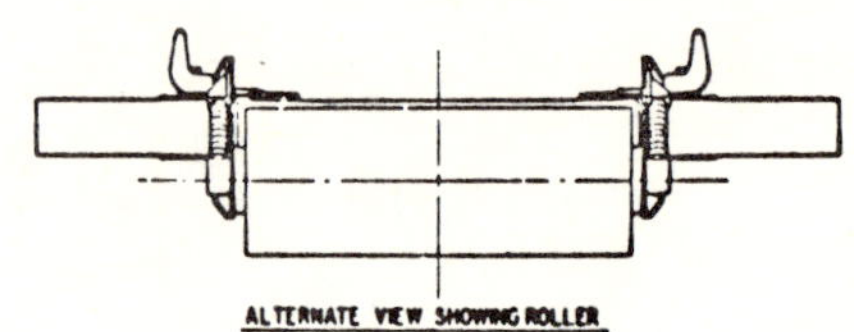

Car, Half-Track, M2 (front)

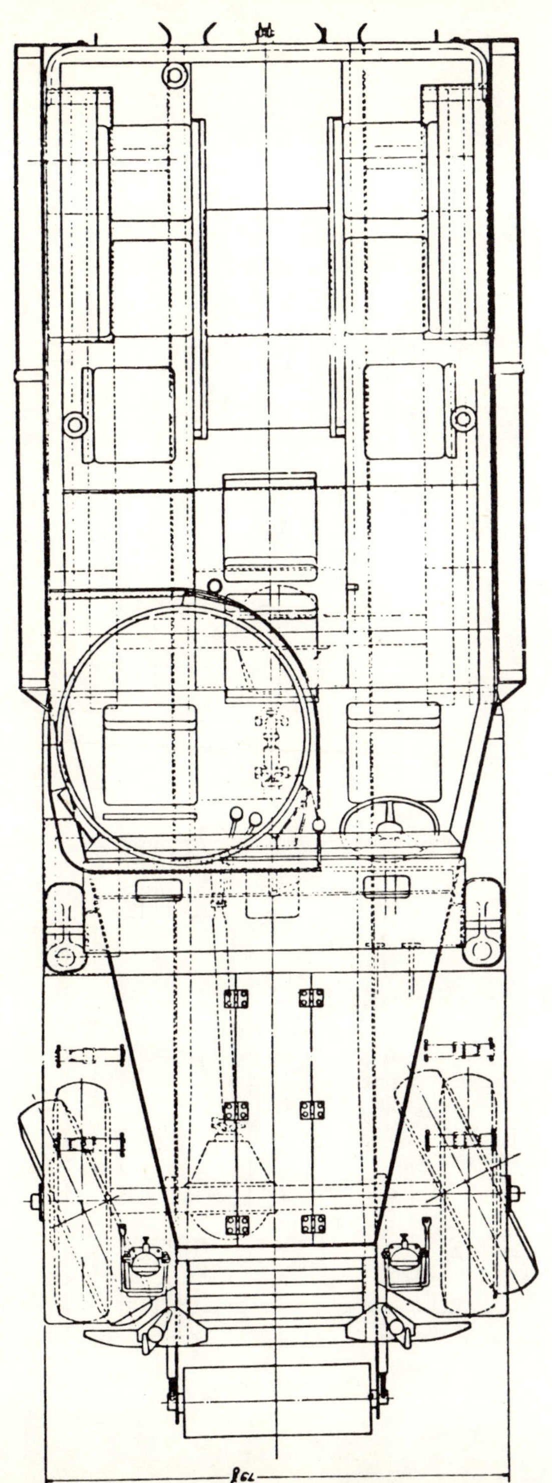

Half-Track Car M9A1 (plan)
(for side elevation see title page)

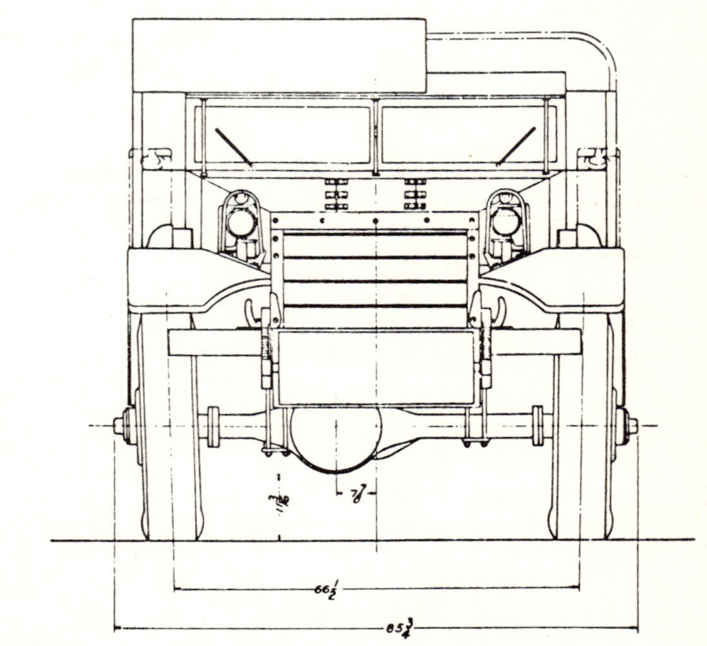

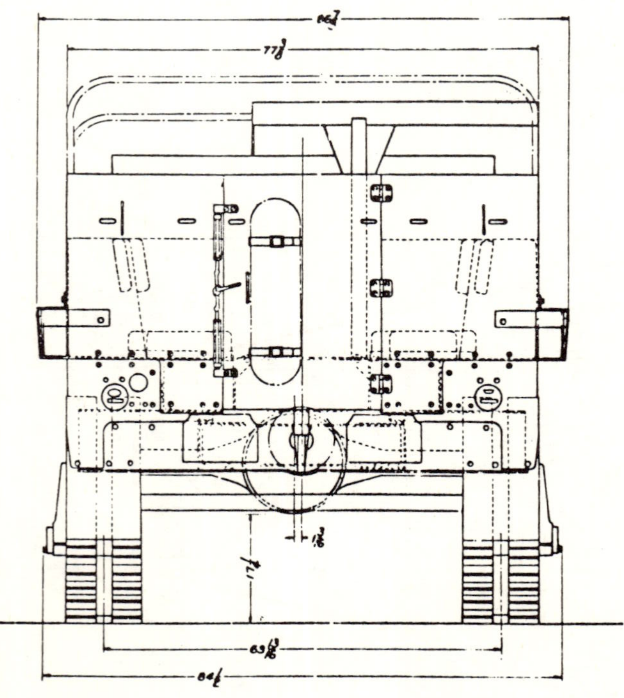

Half-Track Car M9A1 (rear and front)

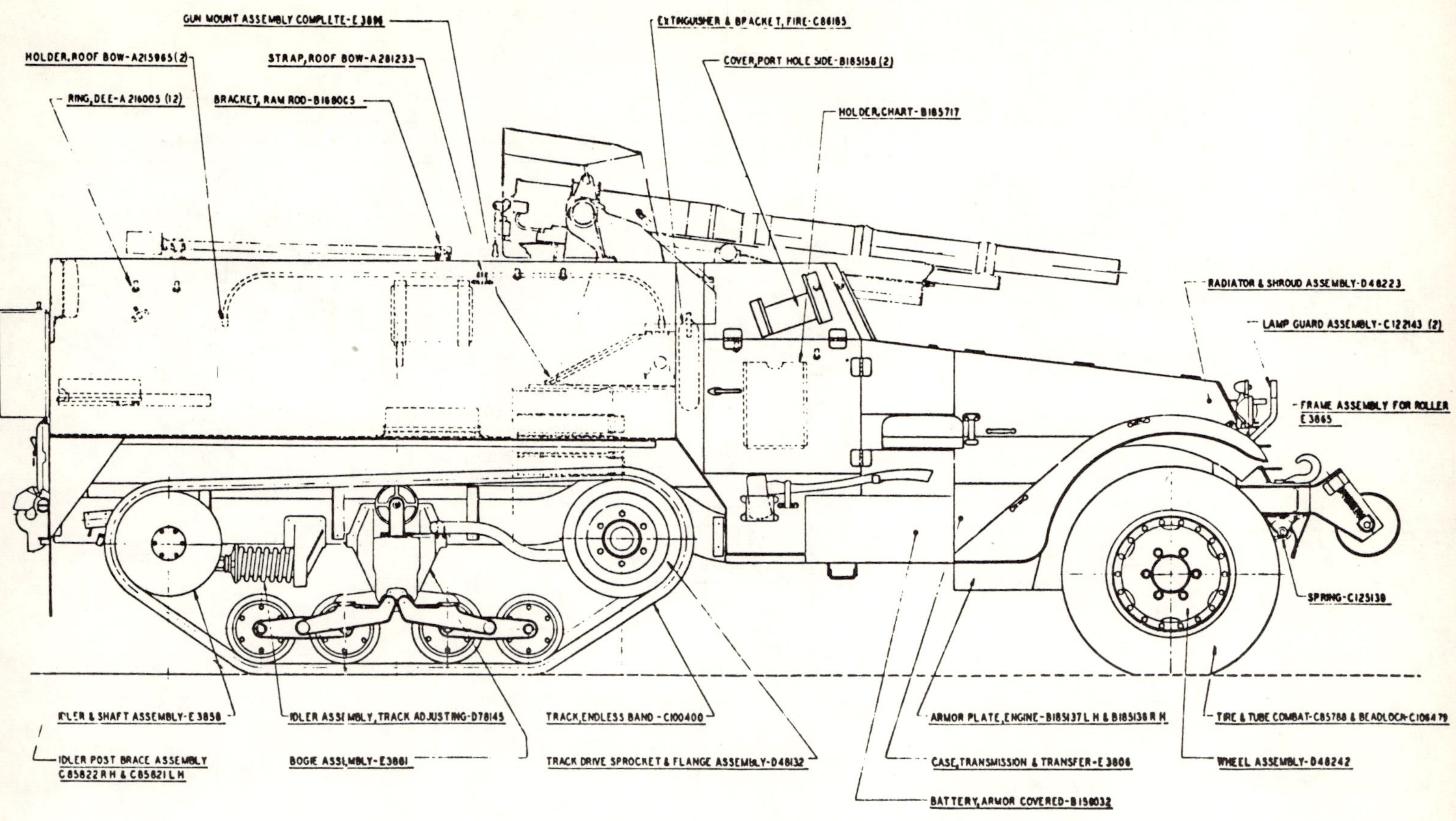

Carriage, Motor, 75mm Gun M3A1 (right side)

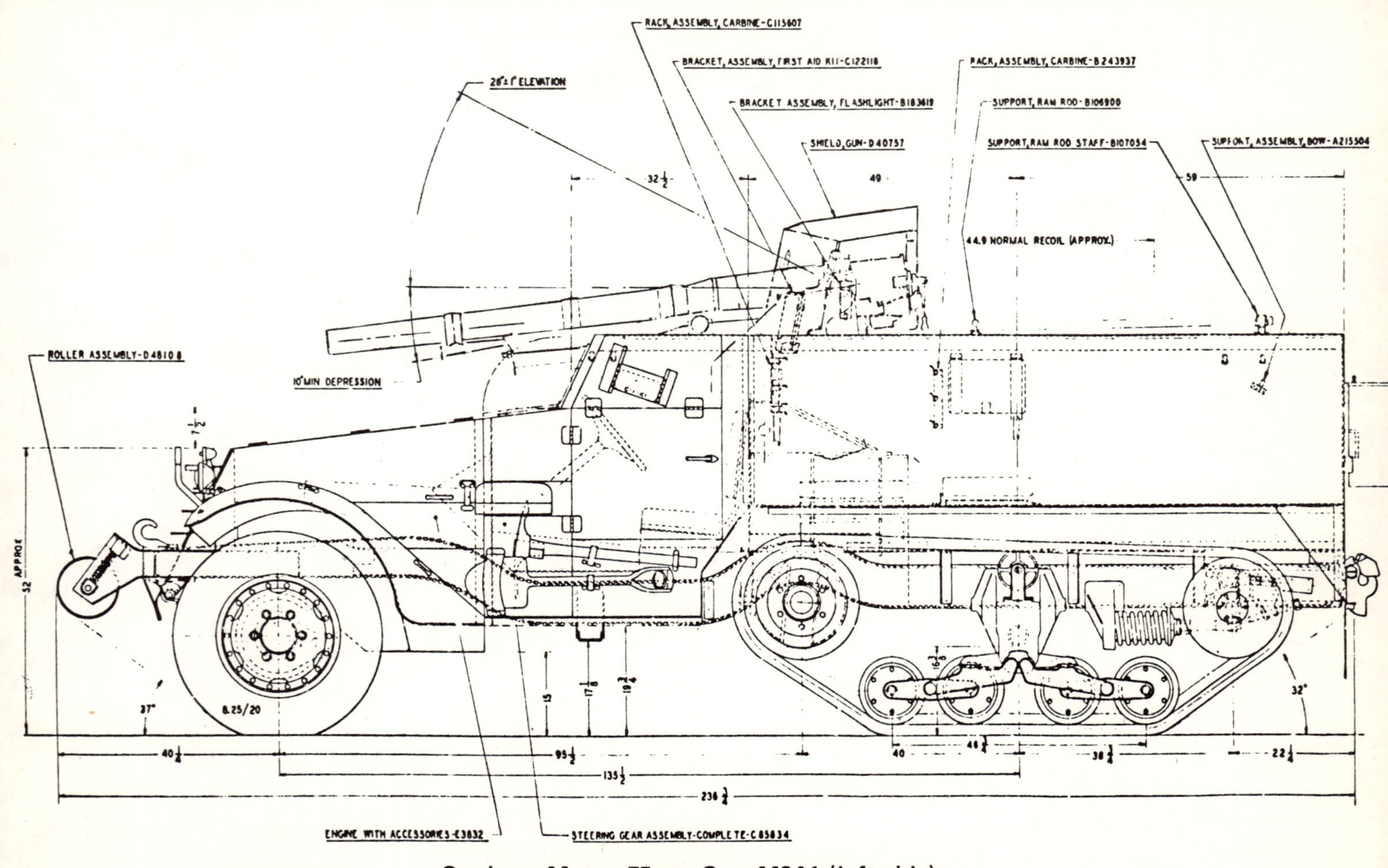

Carriage, Motor, 75mm Gun, M3A1 (left side)

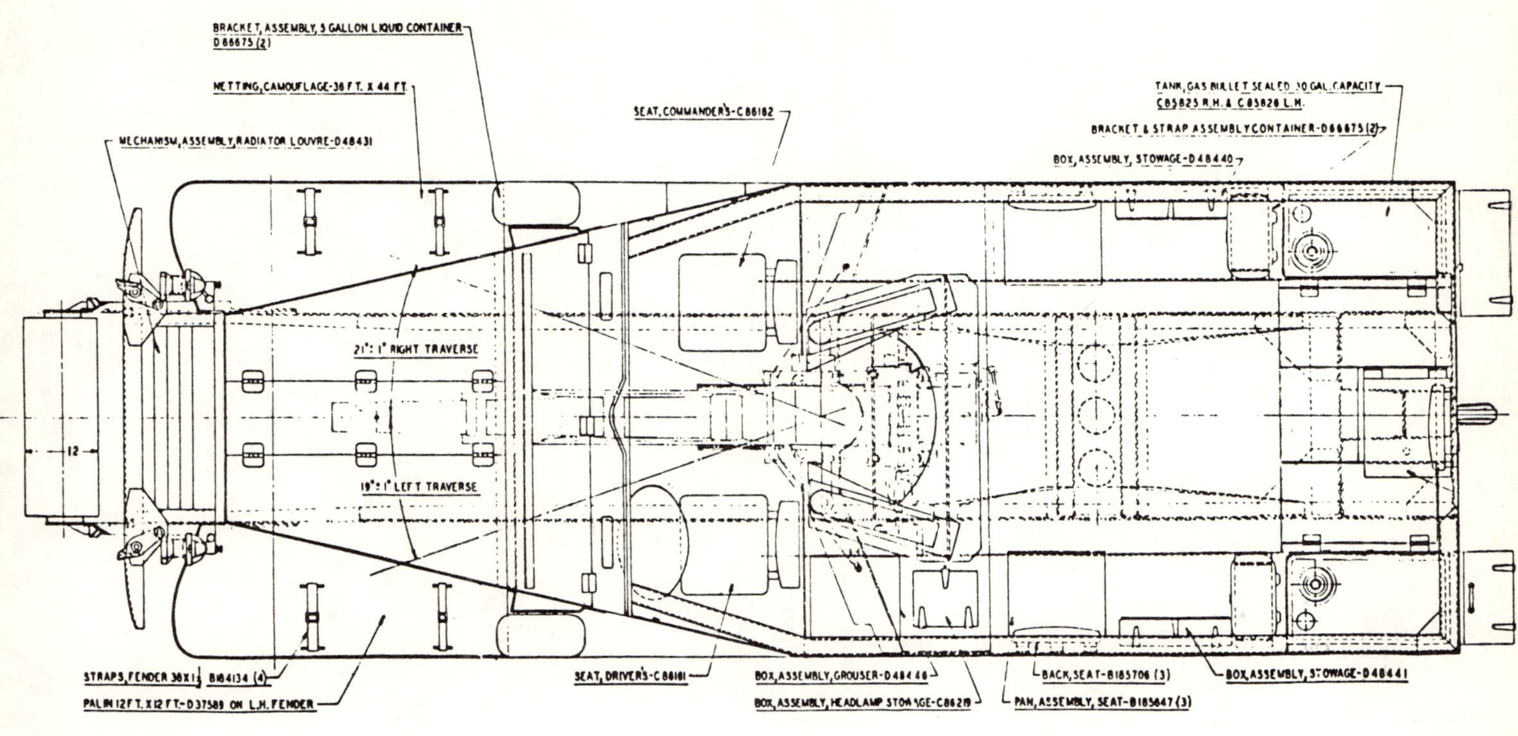

Carriage, Motor, 75mm Gun, M3A1 (top)

Carriage, Motor,
75mm Gun,
M3A1
(front and rear)

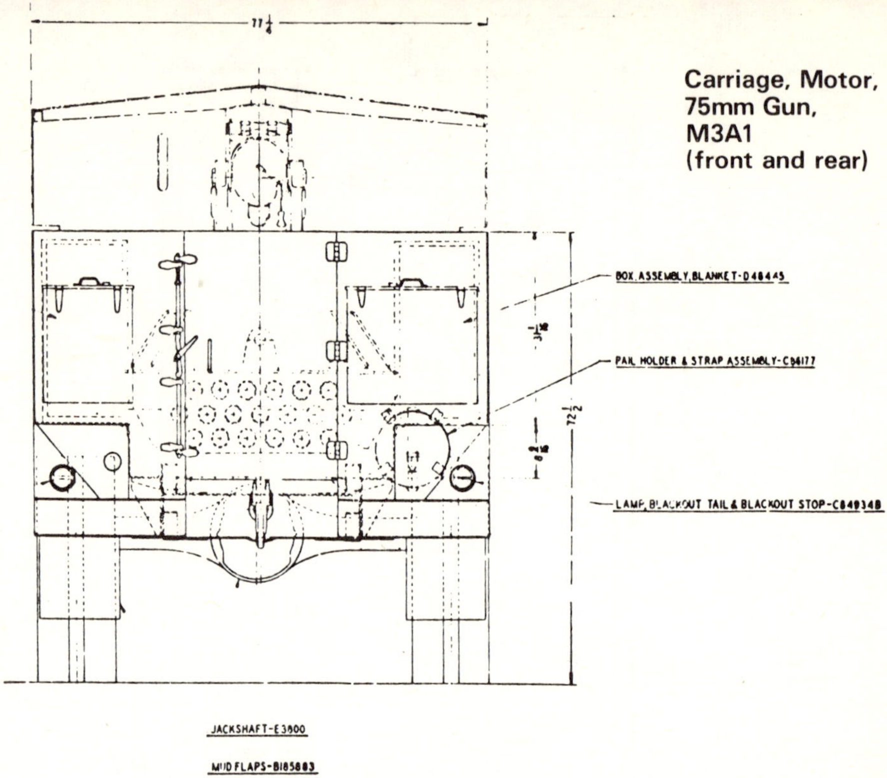

BOX ASSEMBLY, BLANKET-D48445
PAIL HOLDER & STRAP ASSEMBLY-C94177
LAMP, BLACKOUT TAIL & BLACKOUT STOP-C84934B

JACKSHAFT-E3800
MUD FLAPS-B185883

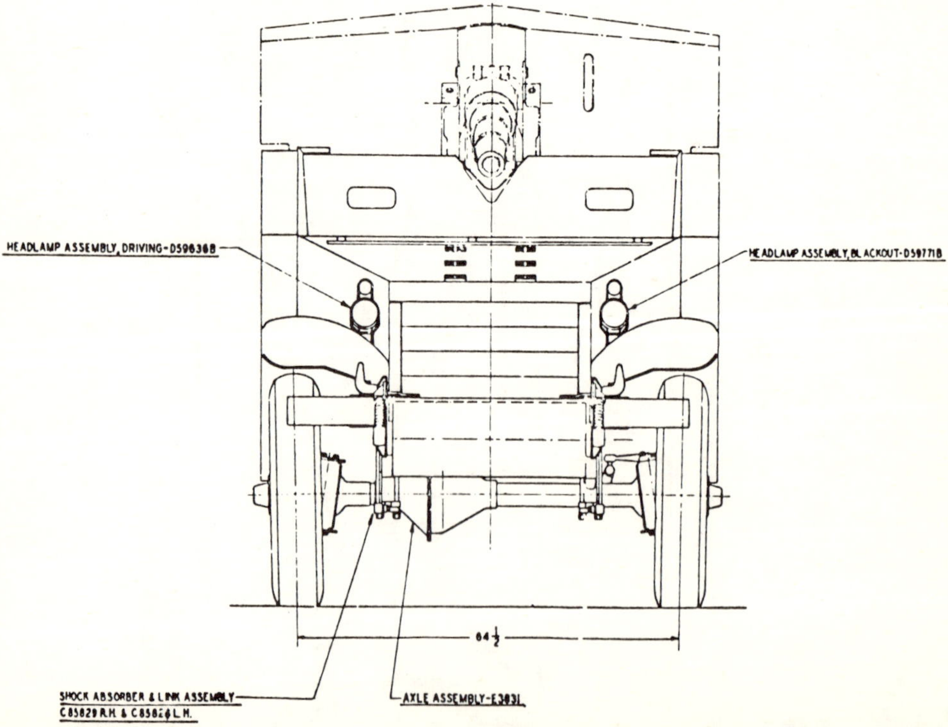

HEADLAMP ASSEMBLY, DRIVING-D59636B
HEADLAMP ASSEMBLY, BLACKOUT-D59771B

SHOCK ABSORBER & LINK ASSEMBLY-
C85829 R.H. & C85826 L.H.
AXLE ASSEMBLY-E3831

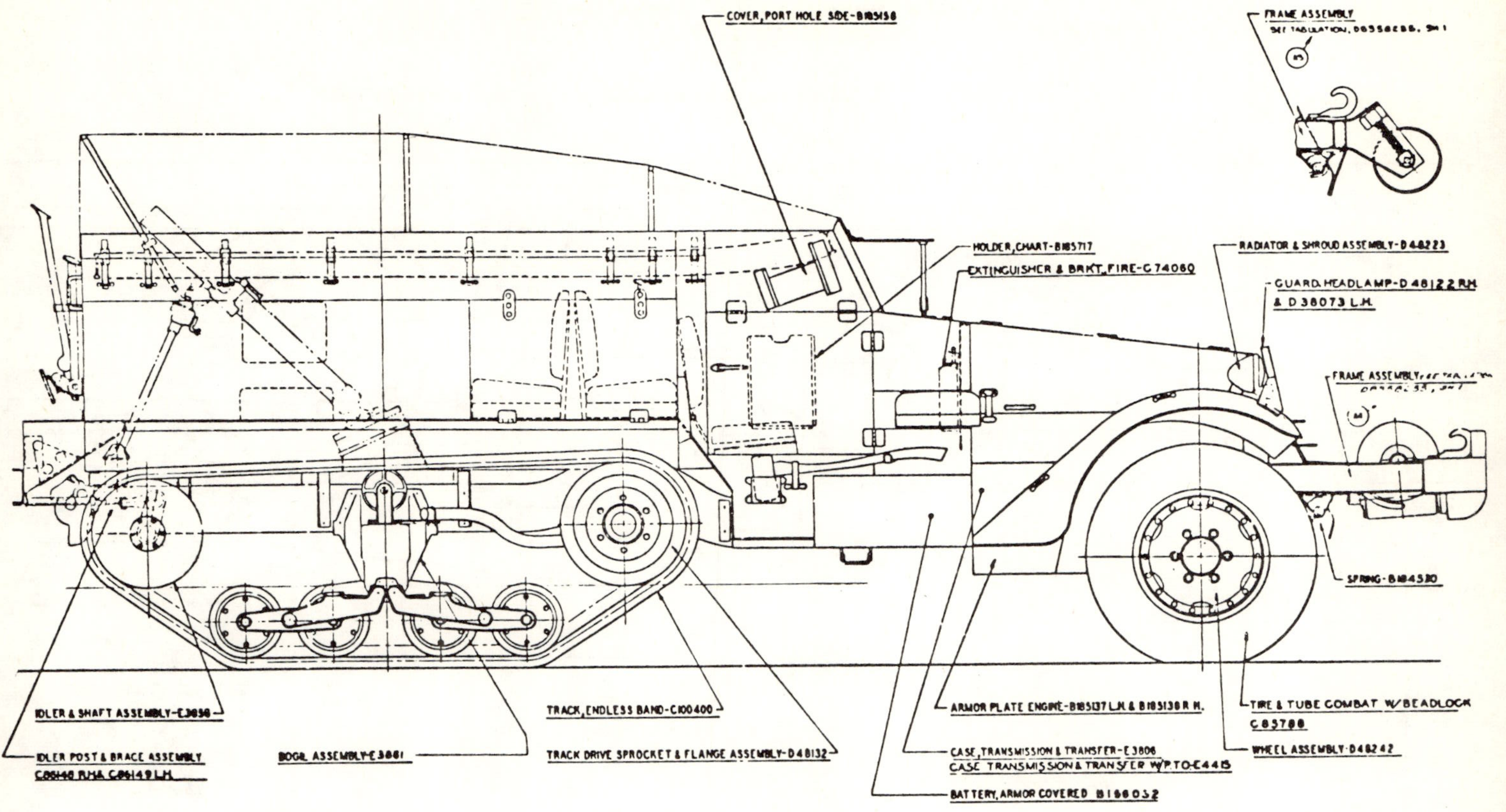

Carrier, Mortar, 81mm, M4 (right side)

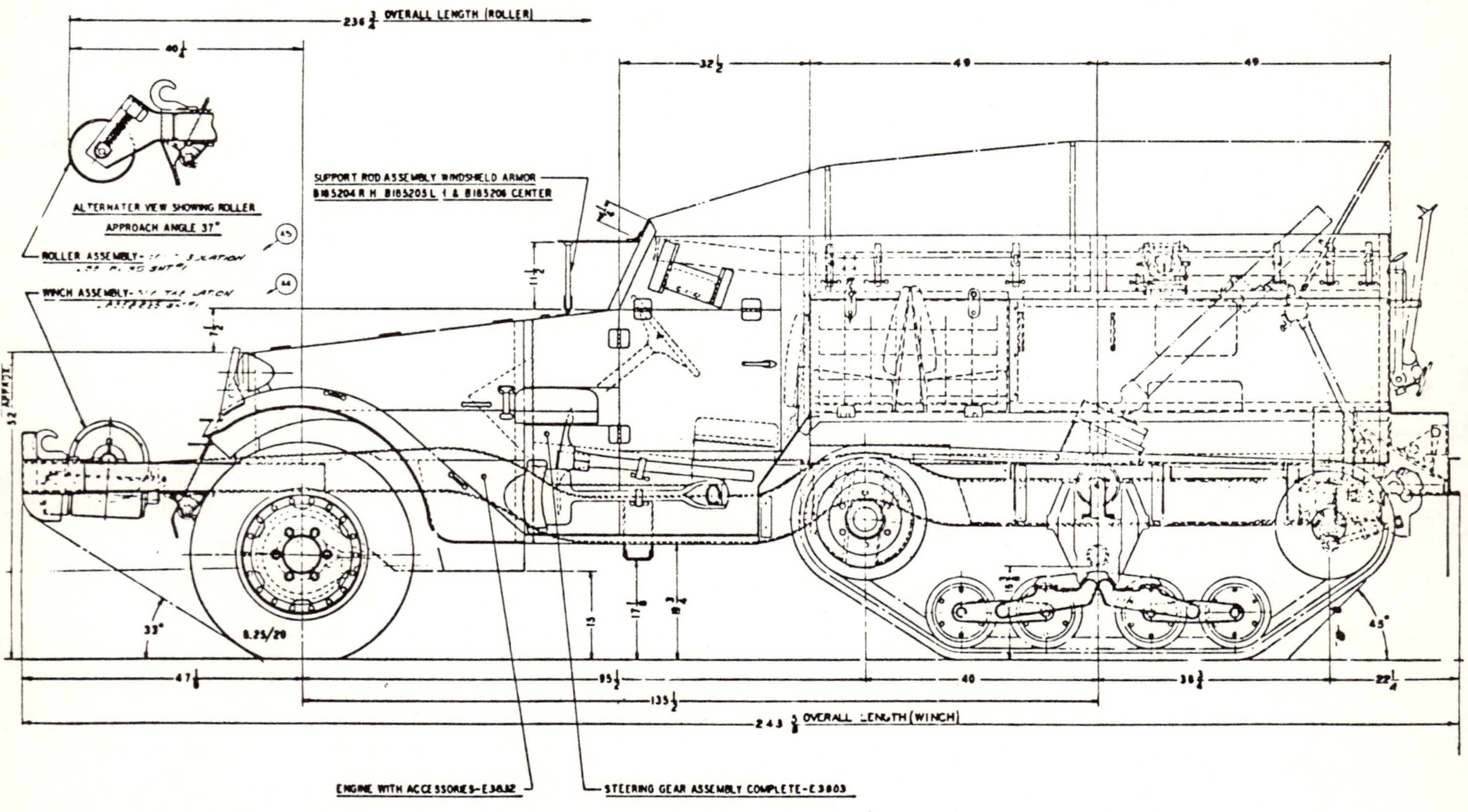

Carrier, Mortar, 81mm, M4 (left side)

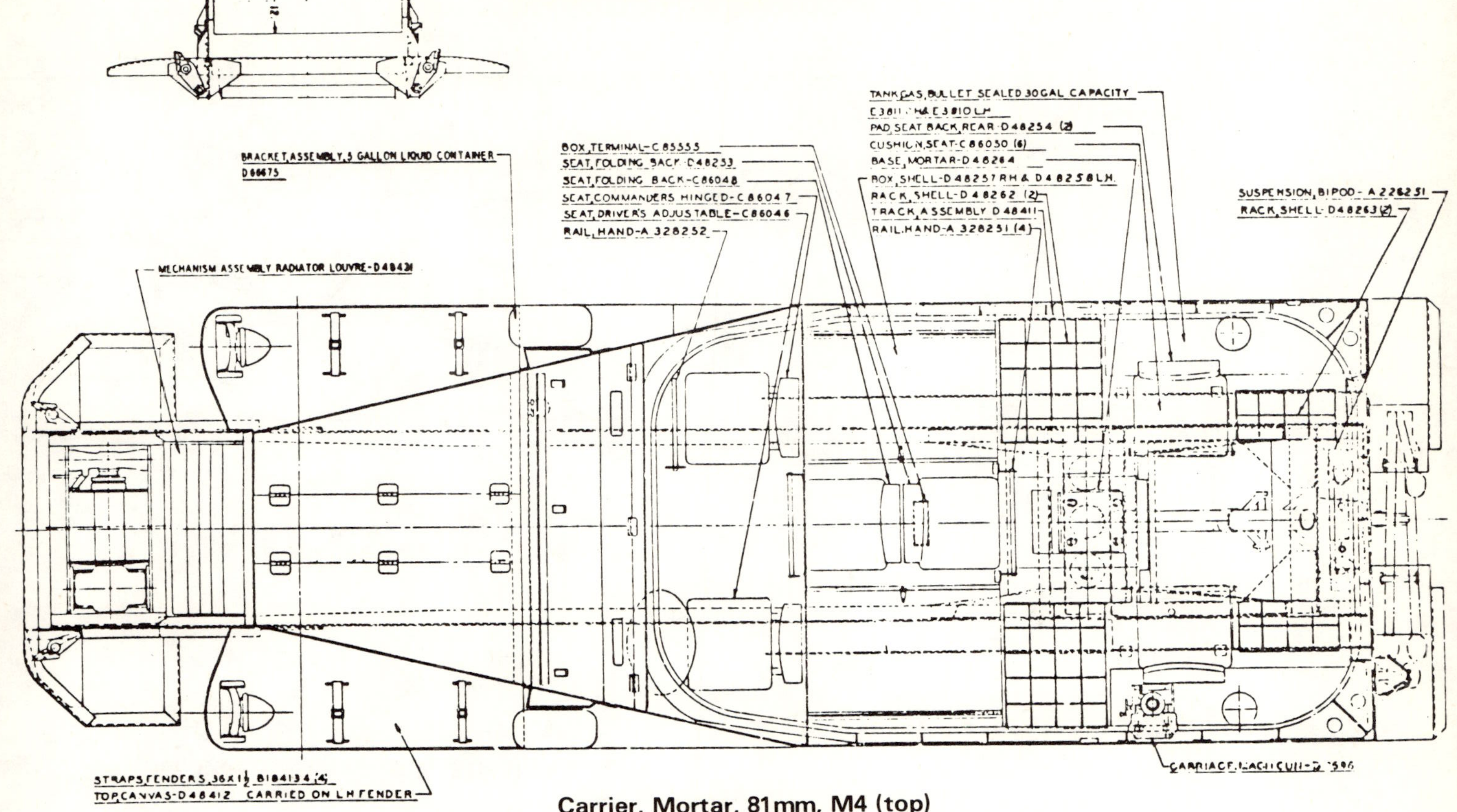

Carrier, Mortar, 81mm, M4 (top)

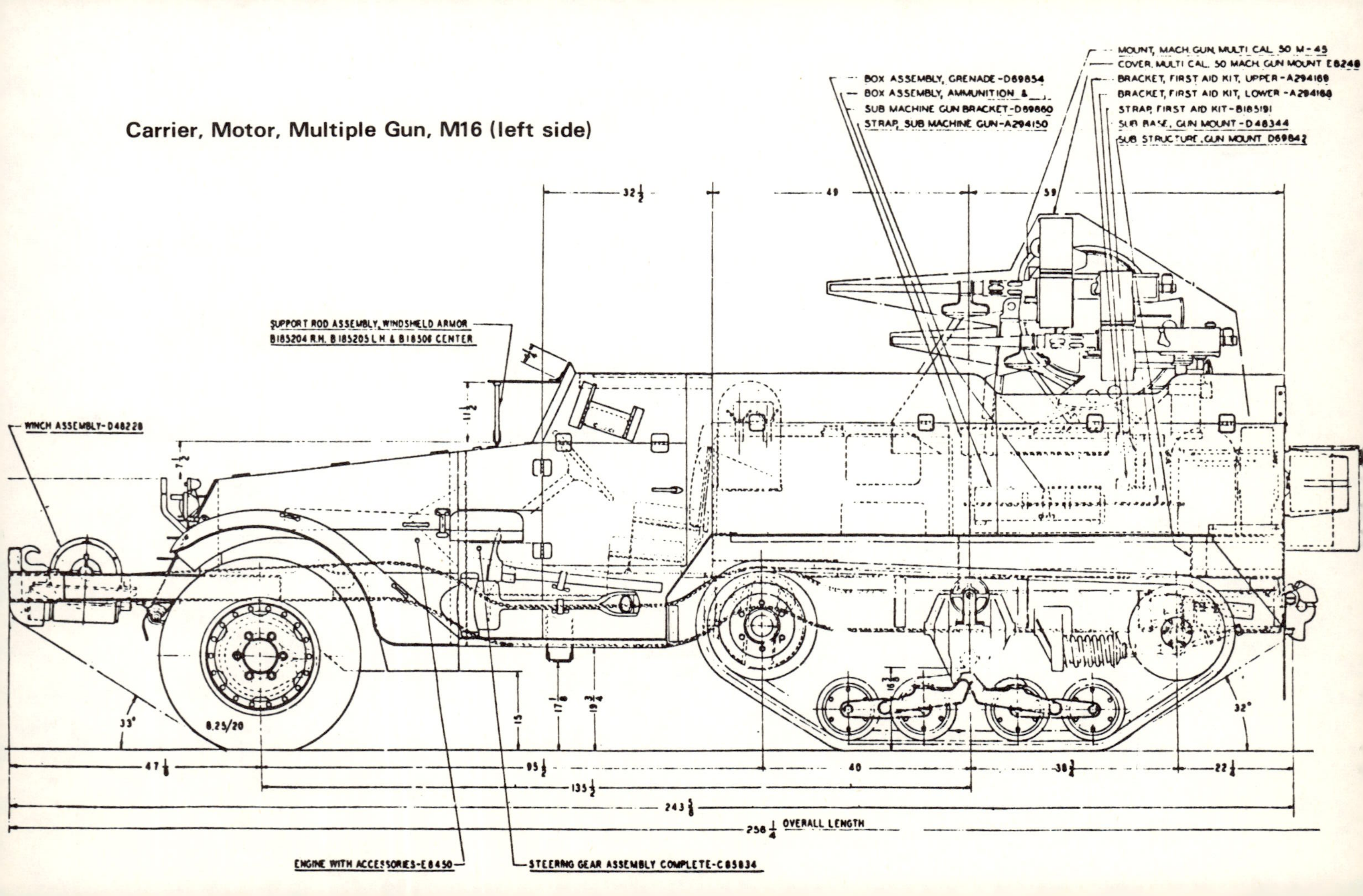

Carrier, Motor, Multiple Gun, M16 (left side)
MOUNT, MACH. GUN, MULTI CAL. 50 M-45
COVER, MULTI CAL. 50 MACH. GUN MOUNT E8248
BRACKET, FIRST AID KIT, UPPER-A294168
BRACKET, FIRST AID KIT, LOWER-A294168
STRAP, FIRST AID KIT-B185191
SUB BASE, GUN MOUNT-D48344
SUB STRUCTURE, GUN MOUNT D69842
BOX ASSEMBLY, GRENADE-D69854
BOX ASSEMBLY, AMMUNITION &
SUB MACHINE GUN BRACKET-D69860
STRAP, SUB MACHINE GUN-A294150
SUPPORT ROD ASSEMBLY, WINDSHIELD ARMOR
B185204 R.H. B185205 L.H. & B18506 CENTER
WINCH ASSEMBLY-D48228
ENGINE WITH ACCESSORIES-E8450
STEERING GEAR ASSEMBLY COMPLETE-C85834
OVERALL LENGTH
8.25/20

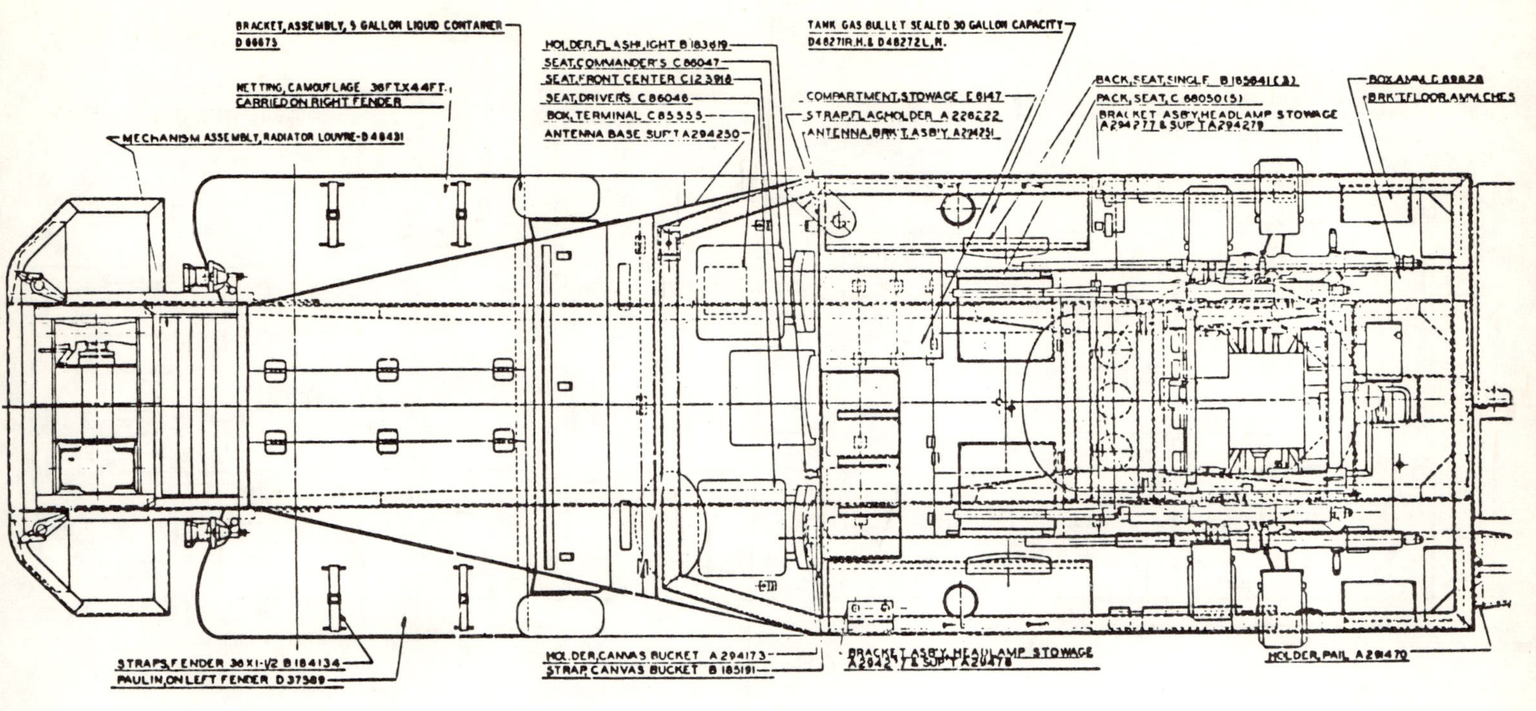

Carriage, Motor, Multiple Gun, M16 (top)

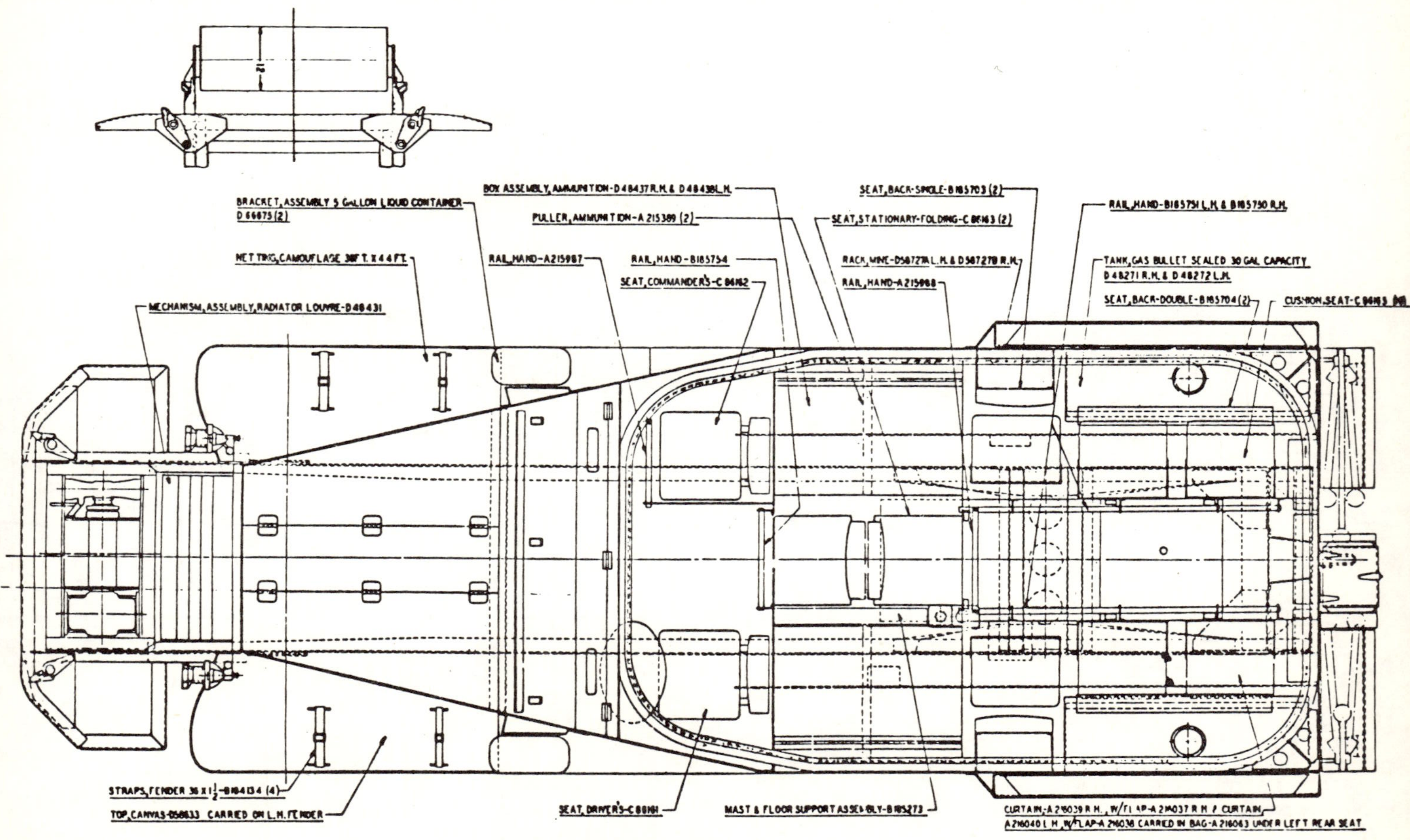

Car, Half-Track, M2 (top)

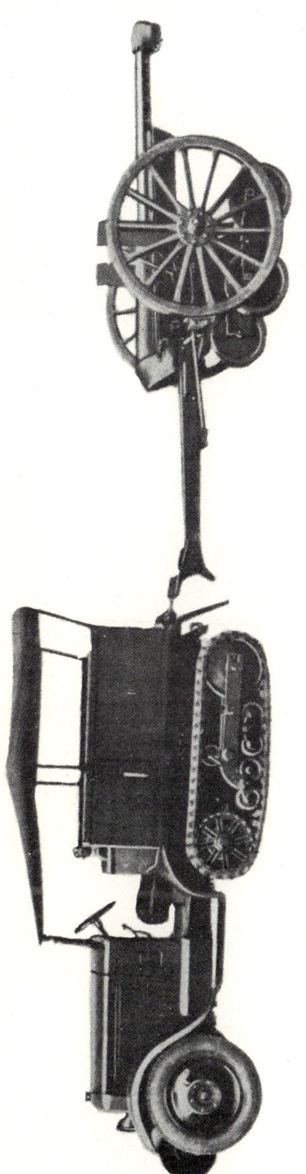

Tracteur Citroen-Kégresse P.17 (with Canon de 75) as evaluated by the U.S. Ordnance Department in 1931.

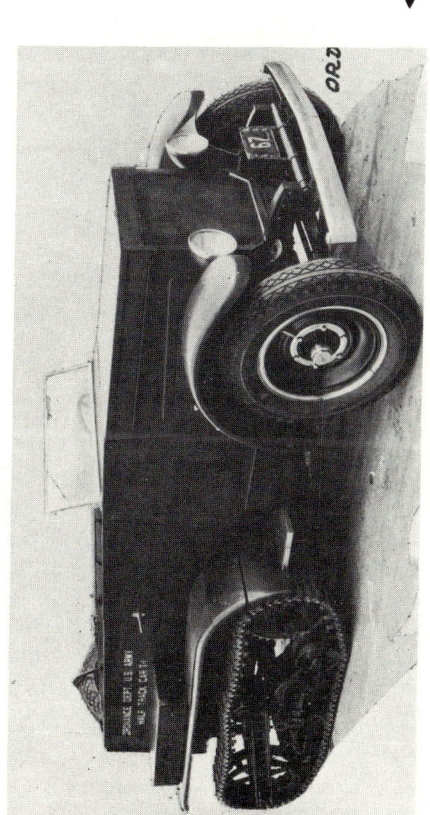

Half-Track Car T1.

Top to bottom: Half-Track Car T1E1 (M1); Half-Track Car T1E3 (note modified suspension); Half-Track Truck T1, 1933.

Above: Half-Track Truck T3, of 1933, was a Linn WD-12 commercial type half-track bought in small numbers as a heavy artillery tractor. Note the winch behind the cab. Note that Half-Track Truck T4 was similar to the T1 shown opposite, but had a line-laying body for Signal Corps use. The T1 and T4 were General Motors vehicles.

Above: Half-Track Truck T5 was another General Motors vehicle like the T1 and T4. 24 were purchased in 1935 as artillery tractors. Note conventional cab doors and Cunningham type half-track bogies.

Above: Half-Track Truck T8 was a Ford truck with Trackson patent cable and chain half-track conversion sets for the rear wheels, tested only. Below: Half-Track Truck T9 with Cunningham Kégresse-type bogie was standardised as Half-Track Truck M2.

Above: Half-Track Truck T9E1 was an experimental variant of Half-Track Truck T9 fitted with light tank type bogies and track to test against the Kegresse-type bogies of the T9. The T9 and T9E1 were built by Marmon-Herrington. Below: The Scout Car M2, built by White provided the body and chassis layout from which the armoured half-tracks were developed.

Above: Half-Track Personnel Carrier T7. Below: Half-Track Scout Car T14.
Bottom: Half-Track Car M2 without winch (note front roller).

Top: Half-Track Car M2 with winch. Note large headlights and no side racks.
Above: Half-Track Personnel Carrier M3 with winch, canvas tilt in place. Note small headlights and fitted side racks.

Above: Half-Track Personnel Carrier M3. Below: Half-Track Car M2E6. Bottom: Half-Track Car M2A1, with winch.

Above: Half-Track Car M2A1 showing .50 and .30 cal. machine guns mounted and vehicle fully equipped.

Above: Half-Track Personnel Carrier M3A1, with winch. All equipment shown stowed.

Above: Half-Track Personnel Carrier M3A1, with winch, showing .50 and .30 cal. machine guns mounted.

Above: Half-Track Car T29, showing under chassis heater equipment on cabside, a feature tested on this vehicle.

Above and below: Three views of Half-Track Car M3A2, pilot model, fully stowed and equipped.

Above: Half-Track Personnel Carrier M5, basic vehicle without winch and not stored or armed.

Above: Half-Track Car M5A2 (T31), fully equipped.

Above and below: Three views of Half-Track Personnel Carrier M5A1, without winch, fully stowed and equipped.

Above: Two views of Half-Track Car M9A1, with winch, fully stowed and equipped. Note the rounded rear corners on the superstructure and the flat section mudguards which identify IHC-built vehicles.

Multiple Gun Motor Carriage T1E1.

Multiple Gun Motor Carriage T1E2, with superstructure sides removed.

Multiple Gun Motor Carriage T1E3.

Multiple Gun Carriage T1E4, standardised as Multiple Gun Carriage M13.

Multiple Gun Carriage M14.

Multiple Gun Carriage T28 (March 1941).

Multiple Gun Carriage T28E1 (July 1942).

*Multiple Gun Motor Carriage M15
(production vehicle).*

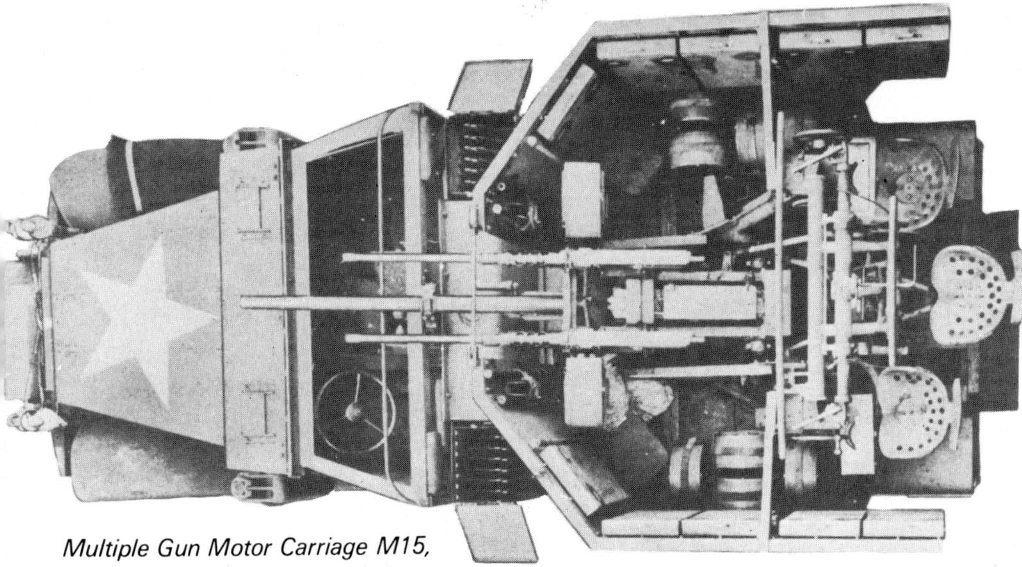

*Multiple Gun Motor Carriage M15,
top view.*

Multiple Gun Motor Carriage M15A1.

Two views of Multiple Gun Motor Carriage T37E1. T37 similar but with guns mounted in square.

Above: Multiple Gun Motor Carriage T58. Vehicle was originally used as T1E2 with earlier armament and is still marked as such. Below: Multiple Gun Motor Carriage M16.

Above: Multiple Gun Motor Carriage M16, rear view. Below: Lend-Lease Multiple Gun Motor Carriage M17 with Soviet troops.

Above: Multiple Gun Motor Carriage T10.

Below: Twin 20mm Gun Motor Carriage T10E1.

Two views of Half-Track Car T16, showing roof in opened and closed position, and modified suspension.

Top: 40mm Gun Motor Carriage T1. Above: 40mm Gun Motor Carriage T54. Below: 40mm Gun Motor Carriage T54E1.

Multiple Gun Motor Carriage T60.

Multiple Gun Motor Carriage T60E1.

Above: 40mm Gun Motor Carriage T59E1. Below: Half-Track Instrument Carrier T18.

40mm Gun Motor Carriage T68.

57mm Gun Motor Carriage T48.

75mm Gun Motor Carrige T12.

75mm Gun Motor Carriage M3.

75mm Gun Motor Carriage T73.

75mm Howitzer Motor Carriage T30; first pilot model lacking shield.

75mm Howitzer Motor Carriage T30; first pilot model with original design of shield fitted.

75mm Howitzer Motor Carriage T30; second pilot model with revised, lower height, shield.

105mm Howitzer Motor Carriage T19; pilot model as originally produced without shield.

105mm Howitzer Motor Carriage T19; pilot model with production type shield fitted.

105mm Howitzer Motor Carriage T19E1, converted from T19 pilot model.

75mm Gun Motor Carriage M3 in service with the Red Army under Lend-Lease, 1944.

81mm Mortar Carrier M4 with mortar at lowest elevation, vehicle not stored.

81mm Mortar Carrier M4 with rear door closed and mortar at lowest elevation.

81mm Mortar Carriage M4 from rear showing mortar, bomb stowage, seats and fuel tanks.

81mm Mortar Carriage M4A1 fully stored, top view shows interior layout.

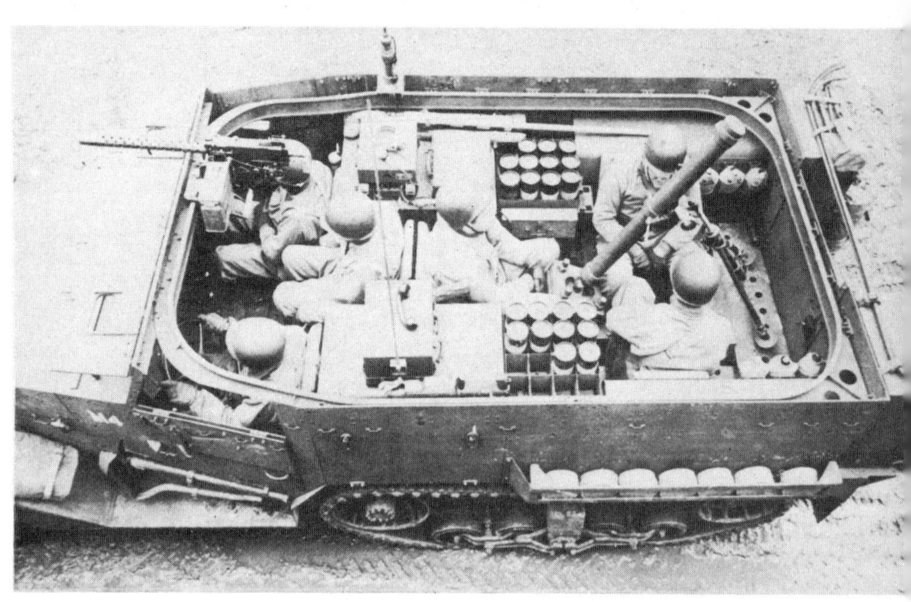

81mm Mortar Carriage M4A1 showing crew positions.

81mm Mortar Carrier M4A1 in action during the Battle of the Bulge, December 1944.

81mm Mortar Carrier M21, fully stored.

81mm Mortar Carrier M21, fully stored and showing interior layout.

Above and below: 4.2 inch Mortar Carrier T21.

Half-Track Truck T3, basic chassis adapted for use with 40mm Gun Motor Carriage T1.

Half-Track Truck T3 with normal armoured superstructure.

Above: Half-Track Truck T16. Below: Half-Track Truck T17.

Below: Half-Track Truck T19.

Experimental Mine Exploder conversion of a M3 Half-Track, with flail attachment.

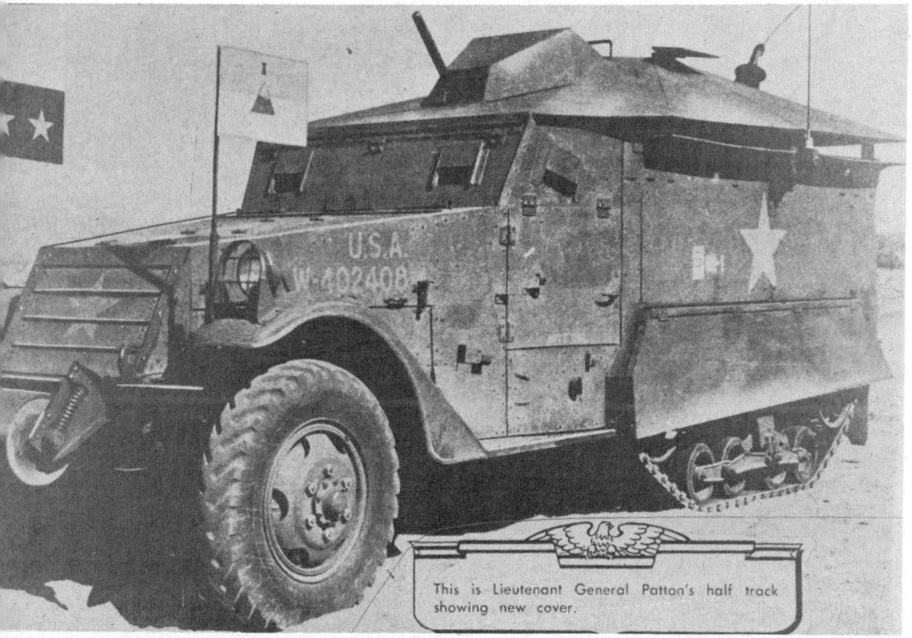

General Patton's personal command vehicle in North Africa, with armoured roof, side skirts, and extra radio equipment. Note divisional and command (2 star general) flags in metal on the wings. This was typical of command car conversions.

Above: Half-Track M2 of the French 2nd Morrocan Division towing a 57mm (6-pdr.) anti-tank gun at the Volturno River, Italy, January 1944. Note the gun armour shields carried on the half-track.

Below: Half-Track M3 of the 8th Army towing a 17 pdr. anti-tank gun at the Gothic Line, September 1944.

Above: Half-Track M5 of the British Army, France 1944, in use as an armoured ambulance.

Right: Half-Track M3 of the US Army in Tunisia carrying a 37mm anti-tank gun, a typical field modification.

Below: Half-Track M2 in Oran with 37mm anti-tank gun in extemporised mount.

Above: Though of poor quality, this view of a M2A1 in Italy shows a typical improvisation – twin .50 cal. machine guns on a raised mount, with a piece of AFV armoured plate as a shield.
Below: Another improvisation – a 75mm Pack Howitzer on a field carriage (less its wheels) arranged to fire from the rear door of a Half-Track M3.

Above: Half-Track M3 in British service, 1961, converted to a wireless vehicle. These post-war British M3s were acquired from USA in 1954-55. Designation: Truck 15 cwt Half-Track, Wireless, M3.

Below: Half-Track M3 in British service, 1958, also converted to a wireless vehicle.

In addition to the M3s acquired in 1954-55, the British also converted some of their remaining wartime issue half-tracks to wireless vehicles in the 1950s. These were originally supplied as Multiple Gun Motor Carriages M14 and had the guns removed on conversion to APCs in 1943-44. The original folding superstructure sections were retained. Above: Vehicle without tilt rails, 1958. Below:Vehicle with tilt rails fitted as wireless office. Designation: Truck 15cwt, Half-Track, Wireless M14. Note rounded rear corners, flat section mudguards.

One of the most extensive of half-track conversions was the British radar range finding and tracking equipment vehicle which was built on the chassis of a M9 or M14.

Above: Complete vehicle with its generator trailer.

Right: Inside of the office body, showing operator and radar display. This saw service into the 1960s.

Above: Half-Track Personnel Carrier M9A1 as supplied to the British Army, 1944-45. This winch-fitted vehicle is shown with the canvas weather cover in place, fitting over the pulpit. British Designation: Truck 15 cwt Half-Track M9.

Below: Last variant in British service was the light recovery conversion used by REME Light Aid Detachments until well into the 1970s. Its jib had a higher lift than that of the FV434 which theoretically replaced it — useful for engine changing as with this Centurion in 1962.

Above: Several types of A-frame jib were fitted to the British light recovery conversions. This close view shows a tubular steel version (compare girder version, opposite page). Note how vehicle winch is utilised. Below: Truck 15cwt Half-Track M9 still in service as an infantry APC on exercises in 1964. Note that 'M9' was used in the British designation even though the vehicle is actually an M9A1.

Half-Track Personnel Carrier M3 of the French Army in Indo-China in 1954. Pulpit removed and replaced by pintle for .50 cal. machine gun. Wire anti-grenade cage added for jungle patrol work.

Battered, but still serving, this is a Half-Track M3 of the South Vietnam Army in 1967, with pintle mounted .30 cal machine guns, each with a shield.

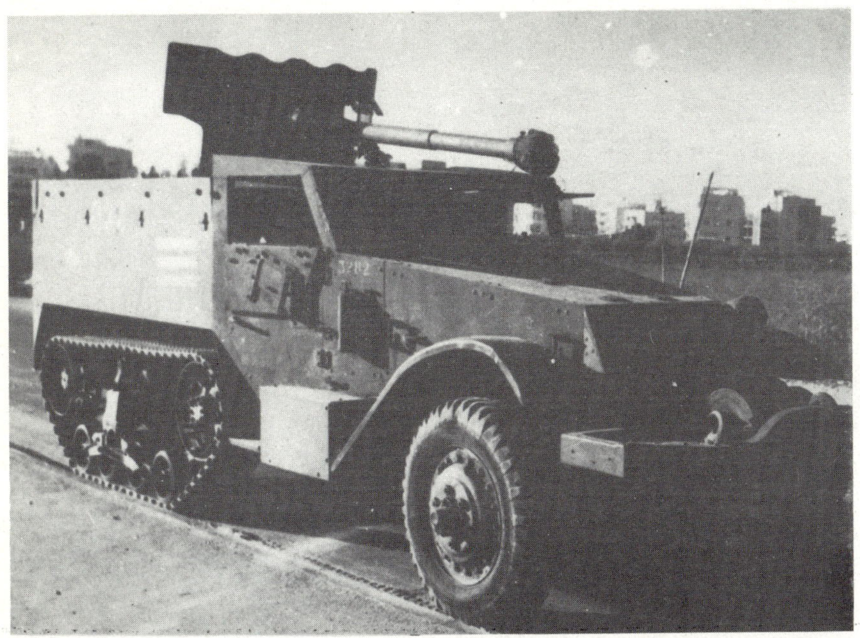

One of the earliest Israeli half-track conversions. This former Multiple Gun Motor Carriage M14 has an ex-British 6 pdr. anti-tank gun less wheels, mounted in place of the multiple machine guns, 1956.

Smartly turned out Multiple Gun Motor Carriages M16 of the Spanish Army in a May 1966 parade.

Two views of a standard Israeli conversion used as a support vehicle for motorised infantry companies. Based on a half-track M14 it features a 20mm gun in an open topped light turret.

Two views of an Israeli anti-tank vehicle conversion of the Half-Track M3. This carries four French SS-11 wire guided anti-tank missiles on a limited traverse launcher, with room for reloads and cover for the crew. These examples are pictured in a 1967 parade.

Israel was a major half-track user in post-war years. Above: Close view of Half-Tracks M3 of a motorised infantry company in the 1967 Six Day War. Note .30 cal machine gun and a .50 cal machine gun on pintle.
Right: Command vehicle conversion of M3 with 'hard' top in Gollan Heights, 1967.

Above: All eyes on the sky as an enemy air patrol is spotted, Italy 1944. Note M1919 Browning .30 cal gun and .50 cal machine gun on this M3.

Below: The Multiple Gun Motor Carriage M16A2 of post-war years.

Above: Multiple Gun Motor Carriage M16 in winter camouflage, December 1944.
Below: Medical Corps Half-Track M3 ambulance evacuates wounded near the front line, Echtz, December 1944.